PLATO

The Midwife's Apprentice

PLATO

The Midwife's Apprentice

by

I. M. CROMBIE

Fellow of Wadham College, Oxford

GREENWOOD PRESS, PUBLISHERS
WESTPORT, CONNECTICUT

Library of Congress Cataloging in Publication Data

Crombie, I. M.
  Plato, the midwife's apprentice.

  Reprint. Originally published: New York : Barnes &
Noble, 1965, c1964.
   Includes index.
   1. Plato. I. Title.
B395.C72 1981   184   81-6812
ISBN 0-313-23243-1 (lib. bdg.)   AACR2

First published 1964 by Routledge and Kegan Paul Ltd.

Reprinted with the permission of Routledge and Kegan
Paul Ltd.

Reprinted in 1981 by Greenwood Press
A division of Congressional Information Service, Inc.
88 Post Road West, Westport, Connecticut 06881

Printed in the United States of America

10 9 8 7 6 5 4 3 2 1

Contents

Preface

I SET OUT, some while ago, to write a short book in which I was to argue that the traditional interpretation of Plato's philosophical position could no longer be taken for granted. By the time I had marshalled the arguments for the views that I wanted to put forward, it had run to over nine hundred pages—hardly the provocative little pamphlet I had intended. Now, however, that the nine hundred pages have been published (by Messrs Routledge & Kegan Paul, in two volumes, under the title *An Examination of Plato's Doctrines*[1]) it seemed that it might be worth trying to put out something much slighter, containing my conclusions only without the arguments on which, it is hoped, they rest. The result is the present book. Lest the reader should suppose that what is set out without argument must be uncontroversial and ought to be believed, may I ask him once and for all in the emphasis of bold type **not to believe one word of this book** unless from his own studies in Plato he sees reason to agree with me? I have not played for safety; there is neither pleasure nor profit to be got from playing safe in Platonic exegesis. What can safely be said about Plato has been said already, often. What I offer is not an account of what Plato said, but one interpretation of its significance.

A word about the figure of the midwife which I have incorporated into my title. She is Platonic all right, but I think I have developed her a little beyond what the texts allow. There is no strict warrant for the close connection I have made

---

[1] References to these volumes are given in the form EPD 1. EPD 2.

between the figure of the midwife and the doctrine of *anamnêsis* or recollection. But I do not think that Plato would have disapproved of what I have done to his simile. Finally in a book of this unscholarly nature acknowledgments might not be entirely tactful. Therefore, while my debts are many they shall be nameless.

I. M. CROMBIE

Oxford, 1963

So if you try subsequently to have another brain-child, Theaetetus—well, if it comes about, the thoughts that you conceive will be better thoughts as a result of the criticism you have just been subjected to; whereas if you remain sterile, you will be aware of your ignorance, and this will chasten you, and make you easier to deal with, and less tedious to your friends.

Socrates in the *Theaetetus*

I

Preliminaries

PLATO was born in Athens in 427 B.C., the son of an aristocratic
family. He lived in Athens for most of his life, and died there
eighty years later in 347. His life was fairly uneventful. He must
have seen military service in his youth in the Peloponnesian
War against Sparta which brought about Athens' political
downfall, possibly also in subsequent wars. He took no part in
Athenian politics, but he was involved, closely for a time, less
closely for a longer period, with the politics of Syracuse. At
some time in his middle life (perhaps in the 380's) he decided
that the contribution which he could make to his city was to
teach, and he bought a piece of land, the "Academy", on which
to found a philosophical school. This appears to have been
something rather like a college in medieval Oxford—a community of scholars, young and old, in which instruction was
given to the young and in which the older pursued their own
studies. Scientific and philosophical speculation was obviously
among the main activities of the Academy, but there is evidence
that it also produced men who were thought qualified to give
advice on political matters such as the devising of constitutions.
It seems in fact to have been a centre of intellectual activity
both theoretical and practical. How close was the relationship
between its members seems a little unclear. A certain agreement
on the general lines of philosophical doctrine appears to have
obtained—roughly speaking members of the Academy were
Platonists—though it is evident that this was not such as to
preclude disputes within the general framework. Aristotle went
to the Academy as a youth and stayed there for some eighteen

years. He certainly heard Plato discoursing on philosophy, though his contact with him may not have been very close; at any rate he does not seem to have put to Plato various questions about the interpretation of his written works which ought to have been easy to settle. Perhaps Plato in his old age was a somewhat unapproachable figure. The Academy, then, in which Plato spent more or less the second half of his life, appears to have been a community of fairly like-minded men, with Plato himself as the source of inspiration; and this, apart from writing, was his main life-work.

What intellectual influences will Plato have been subjected to in his youth? He will have gone to school, and been taught there to read and write and to do elementary arithmetic. At school also he will have been made to study the Homeric poems, which were the common cultural inheritance of the Greeks. From them he will have learnt the traditional myths and legends of the gods and heroes, and the archetypes of noble conduct. On leaving school he will have found nothing like the Academy at which to continue his education. He will, however, have found a vigorous intellectual life around him. From his own writings we learn of the Athenian fondness for philosophical conversation, carried on in public places such as gymnasiums. We learn also of public lectures given in Athens by visiting intellectuals such as Zeno, at an earlier date, or Protagoras. Some of these lecturers will have been simply men of renown who had been prevailed on to expatiate; others will have belonged to the class of professional lecturers known as Sophists. (The Sophists were, generally speaking, itinerant lecturers who charged for admission to their courses, which might be on widely divergent topics, ranging from the proper meaning of words to the whole duty of man).

It was also (Plato's writings suggest) possible, though one gathers it was not so very easy, to get hold of written works by philosophers such as Parmenides, Heraclitus, Anaxagoras and Protagoras. But the greatest influence for any really intelligent Athenian of Plato's generation will probably have been that of Socrates. Socrates was in his forties when Plato was born. He was an eccentric personality—ugly, ungainly, capable of immense physical endurance, given to platonic attachments to young men, argumentative, a challenger of conventions but at the same time an upholder of traditional values, a man who overtrumped the radicals by being, in his conservatism, more radical then they, as indifferent to discomfort as he was capable of heavy drinking, uncompromising in his religious and moral convictions, on those who fell under his influence an irresistible force. Socrates seems to have spent the greater part of his time in philosophical discussion, particularly with the young, and particularly in inquiry into the fundamental assumptions underlying the conduct of life and of public affairs. To what extent he did this simply because he enjoyed it we do not know; but certainly to some extent he did it out of deliberate policy. He was, he said, the city's gadfly, whose duty it was to destroy men's complacent assumptions, and especially to show them that they had a real understanding of nothing. Perhaps he hoped to create a small leaven of dedicated seekers after truth by convincing young men of their own and their elders' very imperfect understanding of the principles they professed. But the effect of his destructive questioning was not always happy. Some of his disciples—Alcibiades in particular—turned out badly, at any rate from the point of view of an unimaginatively patriotic Athenian. In the end, as everybody knows, the Athenians got rid of their gadfly by imposing upon him a sentence of death which he forced them to carry out by refusing to do what it was, no doubt, assumed he would do, namely to escape from Athens. It is hardly possible that Plato could have escaped Socrates' notice, and we are no doubt safe to assume that Plato must have been, occasionally, and probably frequently, subjected to the devastating educational process of a conversation with Socrates. It seems to have left him convinced that it was his vocation to leave behind a permanent record of Socrates' personality.

Nearly all of Plato's writings are in the form of dialogues. The principal exception to this is a batch of thirteen letters, the authenticity of which is disputed by some scholars. Some of the "dialogues" are genuinely dialogues—dramatic representations of philosophical discussion. Others, though written in dialogue form, can be turned into monologues with very little loss. In nearly all the dialogues there is one chief speaker. Socrates is the chief speaker in most of the dialogues; in nearly all the others this office is discharged by an anonymous "Stranger". The view has been held by some scholars that, when Socrates is speaking, what is said is a more or less faithful representation of what was actually believed by the historical Socrates, and that it is only through the mouth of the Strangers that Plato puts forward his own opinions. Others have held that the chief speaker in all the dialogues, whatever he is called, is no more than a mouth-piece for Plato; and of course there are other positions in between. The difficulty for all of these positions— and the difficulty for anyone who attempts to give account of Plato's thought—is that if a man chooses to write dialogues he thereby avoids committing himself to anything said by any of his characters. He thus gives himself some of the liberty of a playwright, and can use this liberty, if he wishes, to put forward ideas which he would not subscribe to as they stand, but which seem to him to deserve an airing, either because they may possibly be true, or because they may be stimulating and provo- cative, or for other less serious reasons. Since Plato seems to have held that philosophizing is essentially something which should be done *tête-à-tête*, and to have put in consequence a low value on written philosophy, it is quite likely that to look for a mouthpiece in his writings is to look for something that is not there. It is on the other hand difficult to believe that he would have put so much artistry into something no more original than the representation of the thoughts of Socrates. If, therefore, we look to the dialogues to learn the opinions either of Socrates or of Plato, we must do so with discretion. In the case of Socrates' opinions, we will do well to be very circumspect; the largest assumption we can safely make is that if, in a dialogue, Socrates seems to put some thought forward seriously, then Plato pro- bably believed that something like this thought was a "legiti- mate development" of Socratic ideas—and even this is probably too much. In the case of Plato himself perhaps the most we can say is that an idea which seems to be put forward seriously in some dialogue, more especially if it is also to be found in, or is implicit in, other dialogues, is something that Plato thought it worth while at that time to put forward for serious considera- tion. It is only if what we thus get adds up to something coherent that we can be reasonably confident that we have discovered what Plato believed. Since most interpreters are agreed that a coherent, though not necessarily static, body of doctrine is to be extracted from the dialogues (however much they disagree about what this doctrine is), the position is not as baffling in practice as it might seem likely it would be.

It is not possible to determine the chronological order of the dialogues with any precision. Elaborate investigations into various stylistic points have, however, enabled us to divide them into two groups, the early and the late; and within these two groups some seem nearer to the border-line than others. In effect, therefore, there are three sets of dialogues—those which are definitely early, those which are definitely late, and those which are neither definitely early nor definitely late, many of which were almost certainly written in the middle period. It is satisfactory that the picture of Plato's intellectual development which we get from this chronology is a coherent one.

The following is a table of those dialogues whose authenticity is fairly generally accepted. They are listed in alphabetical order within each group

Plainly early	Neither plainly early nor plainly late	Plainly late
Apology	†*Cratylus*	*Epinomis*
Charmides	† *Euthydemus*	*Laws*
Crito	*Parmenides*	*Philebus*
Euthyphro	*Phaedo*	*Sophist*
Gorgias	*Phaedrus*	*Statesman*
Hippias Major	*Republic*	(or *Politicus*)
Hippias Minor	*Symposium*	
Ion	(or *Banquet*)	
Laches	*Theaetetus*	
Lovers	† *Timaeus* and	
(or *Rivals*)	*Critias*	
Lysis		
Menexenus		
†*Meno*		
Protagoras		

* = authenticity disputed   † = grouping disputed

A particular problem which confronts the interpreter of Plato takes its start from the bad arguments which are quite often to be met with in the dialogues. Of Plato's logical acuteness there can be no reasonable doubt. He was not simply a profound, poetic thinker with a somewhat primitive logical apparatus. Any careful reader of the *Parmenides*, for example, must be impressed again and again to see how many of the logical perplexities which have troubled and still trouble the most exact metaphysical thinkers have been anticipated by Plato, and how precisely he has stated them. Yet the same writer not infrequently allows his characters to use arguments which are fallacious, and sometimes crudely so. What are we to say then? When we try to conjecture Plato's beliefs from his writings, is it safe to assume that the process of thought by which he came to them must have been reasonably consistent? Or should we allow that it may have been logically pretty vulnerable? Should we argue, as some scholars tend to do, that so exact a thinker cannot have perpetrated fallacies except on purpose, to tease the reader's wits, or to warn him that what is being said is not seriously meant? Or should we say, with others, that a thinker guilty of so many fallacies may have had brilliant insight and profound grasp, but cannot be expected to have argued with any precision?

Probably the truth is in between. The atmosphere of a Platonic dialogue is in many ways so contemporary that we tend to forget how near these writings are to the beginnings of disciplined critical thought. We tend to forget how many of the tools that he wanted to use Plato had to forge for himself. Indeed logic, in the sense of an inquiry into the rules of valid argument, was something the forging of which had to be left to Aristotle. It is therefore not to be marvelled at if there are here and there in the dialogues arguments which Plato thought to be good ones but which we can see to be bad. But this does not mean that the interpreter cannot, generally speaking, safely assume that Plato's thought-processes will have been reasonably logical. This assumption is surely justified. Nobody but a pedant bases an opinion on just one chain of argument. A man of active mind is convinced of what he often arrives at by following different roads, sceptical of that which can only be got to along a single path. Therefore if the pedant makes one mistake he can persuade himself of what he has no grounds for; the man of active mind is not so vulnerable. Plato had his intellectual vices, but it is difficult to believe that pedantry was among them. Therefore to defend the principle that Plato's thoughts must have been by and large coherent we do not need to suppose that the fallacious arguments in the dialogues were in every case put there on purpose (though they clearly were in some cases); nor ought we to let the existence of these fallacious arguments puzzle our wills when we would otherwise wish to argue that Plato cannot have meant so-and-so because it would have been illogical of him to do so.

The Traditional Picture

THE ADEQUACY OR OTHERWISE OF ARISTOTLE'S ACCOUNT OF PLATO'S THOUGHT

ARISTOTLE seems to imply that Plato's ideas derived from two main sources and "conformed closely" to a third.[1] The two sources from which Plato derived his ideas are the teachings of the Heracliteans and the questionings of Socrates; and the doctrine to which Plato closely conformed is that of the Pythagoreans. What, then, are the relevant features in the philosophical outlook of these three?

Heraclitus flourished in the first part of the fifth century. We have nothing but fragments of his writings, and these are very enigmatic. His most original doctrine seems to have been that the universe consists entirely of active beings—"everything is in flux". It was for him a mistake to suppose, as some of his contemporaries tended to do, that change only occurs when something has gone wrong and is, so to speak, trying to get right again. Change, on the contrary, is the order of all things. It is impossible, as he said, to step into the same river twice, because, of course, the water has flowed between the first occasion and the second. What is fairly obviously true of "things" like rivers is equally true, he seems to have believed, of entities which we take to have a better claim than rivers to the status of things or stable substances. It is impossible, so to speak, to kick the same stone twice, except in a manner of speaking, because that which

---

[1] *Metaphysics* 987 a 29 – b 9. EPD 1, p. 32.

I kick on the second occasion is not identical with that which I kicked on the first. The stuff of the stone, no doubt, is undergoing a slow but continuous process of change, and so are its relationships, spatial and otherwise, with the rest of the universe. Heraclitus' world, then, is a world of universal and continuous change, both of change in the literal sense in which growth, attrition, decay, getting hotter, getting drier and so on are changes, and also in the sense of change of relationship to other things. What is beautiful is beautiful only in comparison with certain things, or in certain settings; it "changes" and becomes ugly if you compare it to something else, or put it somewhere else; what is old is only so in contrast with something younger; A will only remain near to B so long as neither A nor B moves. What seems to persist only does so because the changes that have taken place in it are not gross enough to have attracted our attention. If there is any genuine fixity in the world it can only be in the patterns to which some changes conform. There are no stable things. It follows that common language is pretty inept for philosophical purposes; for it certainly implies that there are.

Socrates, Aristotle tells us, sought for definitions, and did so "because he wanted to syllogize".[1] What this seems to mean is that he tried to discover what this or that property or kind of thing essentially is, and that he did so because he wanted to discover the framework of necessity—of "things that cannot be otherwise"—which determines what can and cannot happen in the universe.

If Plato had been convinced by a disciple of Heraclitus of the instability of all things, and had then become persuaded of the importance of Socrates' search for definitions, he would have had to do something to accommodate the two. For if it is possible to determine what beauty, say, or knowledge essentially is, then beauty and knowledge must surely be something stable. A belief in essences precludes a belief in complete instability.

In historical fact, Aristotle tells us that Plato was persuaded of Heracliteanism by a Heraclitean *ultra*, namely Cratylus; and it is obvious from the dialogues that Plato revered Socrates, both as man, and as thinker. How intimately he knew Socrates we cannot tell. Socrates was put to death in 399 at the age of

---

[1] *Metaphysics* 1078 b.

seventy, when Plato was twenty-eight, for "corrupting the young and introducing new divinities"—a most impious accusation as Plato calls it in the Seventh Letter. But if Plato was not fairly well acquainted with Socrates, then the element of bluff in the dialogues is remarkable. We can assume, then, that Heraclitus and Socrates were two forces which acted upon him, and that, if he believed in both of them, he must have found it necessary to accommodate them to each other. There is one way of reconciling the notion of universal instability with the notion of definable essences which is fairly obvious, and which is, doubtless, that which Aristotle supposed Plato to have taken. This way consists in separating sharply things from essences, and saying that while things, individuals or particulars are radically unstable, essences or universals are totally change-less. We thus get the world of essences or forms[1] on the one hand which are changeless, intelligible, definable, about which we can and must be precise; and, on the other hand, the world of particular things which are changing, inconstant, indefinite and about which we can only speak in language which is pragmati-cally adequate but philosophically inept, because it implies that there are stable entities. It is even misleading to speak of the world of particular things—let alone the world of cats and dogs, chairs and tables—for if, in the world revealed by our senses, nothing exists but a kaleidoscopic flux, then nothing exists in that world which can deserve the title of "things". The soundest beliefs, therefore, about the physical world can only belong to what Parmenides called the way of opinion—that strange delusion that clouds the minds of all who do not rely exclusively on abstract thought, the minds of all of us most of the time. Knowledge is something that we cannot have of any-thing but essences, universals or forms; and this knowledge can only be acquired by eschewing the use of the senses and relying solely on the mind. Perhaps, however, the two worlds, the world of knowledge and the world of opinion, the world of essences and the world of (by courtesy) "things", can be brought into some degree of relationship to each other. Perhaps we can say that there are sound and unsound opinions and that

[1] "Form" is a translation of the technical term used by Aristotle to denote the changeless entities which, he tells us, Plato believed in. "Idea" is also sometimes used for this purpose, but has misleading associations.

it is a sound opinion that many of the contents of the world are to all intents and purposes, for longish periods, reasonably stable, reasonably like and reasonably unlike certain others, reasonably close to being things; and perhaps we can suppose that the reason why this is so is that the realm of timeless essences is not entirely sundered from the world revealed by our senses; the former perhaps exercises some kind of pull upon the latter, bringing it into some kind of order. There are of course, we concede to Heraclitus, no things of determinate kinds in the world; but on the other hand, we concede to common sense, for all practical purposes it is pretty much as if there were. Perhaps this is so because the world revealed by the senses somehow strives to be like the world of timeless essences, to participate in its clarity and stability, to share its sharpness of edge. Perhaps if there exist to all intents and purposes trees and animals, tables and chairs, things having a moderate degree of stability, the reason why this is so is that there exist, in the realm of essences, essences such as that of tables, and that the bits of semi-congealed flux that we refer to as tables owe their semi-congealed condition to the fact that they "partake" in this essence, imitate it, strive to be like it. If this is so, there will be, then, the world of things which can be known, consisting of essences or universals, and the world of things revealed to our senses and accessible only to the way of opinion, which it is not quite a delusion, as Parmenides implied, to believe in, for it gives us the best approximation there can be to truth about a world which possesses a reasonable degree of stability and determinateness, but which owes these features to the pull exercised by the intelligible realm upon that which would be, otherwise, totally amorphous and inconstant.

When he says that Plato's views derived from the theories of Heraclitus and the practice of Socrates, Aristotle certainly means to attribute to Plato something like the accommodation between these two forces that we have sketched in the previous paragraph. Aristotle says also that Plato's views conformed closely to those of the Pythagoreans.[1] What does he mean by this? The best known doctrine of the Pythagoreans is doubtless the doctrine of transmigration of souls. But Pythagoreanism was

---

[1] Pythagoras flourished in the end of the sixth century, and his disciples persisted as a sect down to Plato's time.

not simply a religious doctrine; rather it was a compound of religion, mathematics and metaphysics. There was indeed the doctrine of transmigration, the doctrine that at or after my death the soul that has animated me may subsequently animate some other creature, human or otherwise. This doctrine carries with it belief in the immortality of the soul (or at any rate the belief that it is not necessarily mortal); and it also seems to carry with it the belief that the soul is something distinct from the body and merely temporarily lodged in it. For it is difficult to see how I could wonder whether the soul that inhabits that bird might haply be the soul of my grand-dam unless that which gives a soul its individuality is neither the body which it animates, nor the experiences which it can recall (for we do not remember the events of our previous incarnations). A transmigrationist therefore seems to be committed to the view that souls are distinct things whose individuality is constituted neither by the body which, from time to time, they animate, nor by the personal existence which they exercise while in a body.

The Pythagoreans were also mathematicians. They discovered the theorem named after their founder, and they began the study of acoustics by finding out that there is a constant and arithmetically simple numerical relationship between the lengths of string needed to produce notes the interval between which is musically concordant. (In the case of notes an octave apart one string is twice the length of the other, and so on). It may have been this discovery that led them to their other well-known doctrine that "things are made of numbers". For it is a bold but intelligible extrapolation from the discovery that arithmetically orderly relations underlie musically orderly relations to conjecture that wherever there is any kind of order and determinateness, there is also numerical order. The doctrine, however, that things are made of numbers seems originally to have gone rather further than this. The Pythagoreans appear to have believed that the stuff of the world is what they called *to apeiron*, the boundless, the indefinite, the indeterminate, the infinite; and that where there are things these consist of what they called pebbles or units. One can think of the boundless as something like Newtonian absolute space, and one can think of pebbles as something like points; only the pebbles have to be not merely geometrical points (for things are made of them), they have to be rather "physical points", points and atoms at once; and they also have to be the units of which numbers consist. This doctrine, however, was damaged in the earlier part of the fifth century, largely by the criticisms of Parmenides and Zeno, and in particular by the discovery of incommensurables. (This is the discovery that, if there is a whole number of units of length in the side of a square, then there is not a whole number of the same units in its diagonal. Since the Pythagorean pebbles were units and hence, they thought, indivisible, this is unfortunate because it means that whatever the size of the pebbles out of which you build the sides of an isosceles right-angled triangle, you cannot build the hypotenuse out of the same pebbles). This discovery destroyed the primitive literal interpretation of "things are made of numbers", for the bricks out of which numbers are made could no longer be identical with the bricks out of which geometrical figures are made; and doubtless the Pythagoreans fell back on some vaguer understanding of the slogan like that which we gave first. Mathematical relationships remained somehow the key to the orderliness of the universe, the boundless being responsible for the rest.

When Aristotle tells us that Plato's ideas resembled those of the Pythagoreans he probably means the resemblance to cover the religious as well as the metaphysical doctrines. It is not easy to see how Plato could have arrived at a doctrine of the soul similar to that of the Pythagoreans as a result of trying to accommodate Socrates to Heraclitus, unless perhaps Socrates' interest in human beings as moral agents had led Plato to think that human persons at least must be genuine unities (and not mere courtesy unities like rivers), that human persons, therefore, were not just patterns in the flux, and that they were or comprised entities of a distinct, non-physical kind. But of course we do not have to suppose that all of Plato's beliefs were arrived at by trying to reconcile Socrates with Heraclitus. So far as the metaphysical doctrines are concerned, the resemblance between Pythagorean doctrines and those which we took Aristotle to be attributing to Plato is obvious enough. In both cases the stuff of the physical universe is something indeterminate, and in so far as there is any determinateness in it this is due to the imposition upon it of intelligible entities or relationships. There would remain, however, an important difference between Pythagorean notions and the "Platonism" which sharply divorces the intelligible from the sensible realm in order that Socrates may define the contents of the former and Heraclitus consign the contents of the latter to eternal flux. This is that according to Pythagoreanism (in its primitive form at any rate) things *are* orderly and intelligible, since they are made of numbers, whereas according to "Platonism" things only *aspire* to be orderly and intelligible, and that which *is* orderly and intelligible is not immanent in physical things, but is related to them rather as the ideal or pattern in which they "participate"—in the sense that they try, though unsuccessfully, to conform to it.

To what extent it was reprehensible of Aristotle to give us the impression that "Platonism" does justice to Plato's metaphysics it is hard to say. It seems to me impossible for one who reads Plato's writings with an innocent eye to suppose that justice is done. To be sure if one approaches the dialogues expecting to find "Platonism" in them it is fatally easy to catch echoes of it, at any rate, in many places; and certainly there is one dialogue, the *Timaeus* (a peculiar and exceptional dialogue on any account), in which we find more than echoes. But an unprejudiced reader cannot really feel that Aristotle's picture of Plato's thought is anywhere near adequate. Perhaps the chief difficulty can be put like this. Almost the strongest impression that we get from Plato's writings is that in philosophy what seems simple and straightforward is always problematical. His genius is in finding hidden difficulties in what people have taken to be clear. Yet what could be more problematical than the doctrine of the two realms? It solves nothing, unless it be the problem of how to reconcile Socrates with Heraclitus; and even this problem could be more simply solved by pruning Heracliteanism of its extravagances, as Plato in fact prunes it in the *Theaetetus*. Heraclitus after all is not gospel. It seems impossible that a mind so sceptical and questioning as Plato's could have been induced, by a juvenile initiation into Heracliteanism, to rest content with a doctrine which represents the physical world as a realm of unstable becoming, accessible only to opinion, and owing such determinateness as opinion finds in it to the fact that it strives to imitate the entities belonging to the wholly other realm of the intelligible. Plato, in fact, could not have thought that "Platonism" was a satisfactory solution of anything. It is possible, however, that "Platonism" will do well enough as an impressionistic sketch of the general tendency of Plato's thought (and to be fair to Aristotle he does not offer it as more than this). It is also possible that Plato in his old age may have seemed more of a "Platonist" than his writings depict him as being. When Aristotle knew him his philosophical conversation may have lost its spring, and on topics which did not currently interest him he may have tended to put forward his opinions rather parrot-fashion. The *Laws* (almost certainly his latest work) contains some brilliant things but it also shows signs of hardening of the mental arteries; in particular it is concerned chiefly with matters of practice, and tends to be impatient with philosophical niceties. It is perfectly possible that in the last decade of his life Plato's account of his metaphysical beliefs tended to be rather perfunctory, and that Aristotle's account of Plato is in consequence an account seen through an old man's spectacles.

Be that as it may, we who did not know Plato in his sixties and seventies, and cannot assume that Aristotle is an absolutely faithful witness, must base our impression of Plato's thought on what we read in the dialogues. What is there that we find there to which Aristotle does not do justice in the sketch that we have been considering?

It will be useful to begin by asking to what extent Aristotle's brief account of Socrates' interests agrees with the interests of Socrates as we find him in Plato's dialogues. Aristotle says that Socrates' primary interest was in ethics, and that he sought for definitions because he wanted to syllogize. The Platonic Socrates is not exclusively interested in ethics, but doubtless his primary interest lies there. That he sought definitions because he wanted to syllogize is an illuminating remark about the Platonic Socrates as he appears in at least one dialogue, namely the *Phaedo*. For here Socrates does seem to put forward the principle that in order to determine what can and cannot happen to an X thing one must first settle what it essentially is to be X: one must define in order to discover necessary connections.[1] You must

---

[1] EPD 2, p. 163 sq.

settle what a soul essentially is before you try to say whether it can or cannot die; when you see that a soul is that which brings life you are in a position to conclude that it cannot. But in other dialogues, if Socrates is seeking for definitions in order to syllogize, then he keeps this ulterior purpose pretty dark. He does indeed seek definitions; he buttonholes somebody and asks him to say what courage or goodness or knowledge or beauty is; and he sometimes says that one cannot proceed to questions of the form "Is S P?" (for example "Is virtue teachable?" or "Does learning to fence make one brave?") without first answering the question "What is S?" ("What is virtue? What is bravery?"). He does not mean by this either that one must settle the linguistic question what the word (say "bravery") means, or the moral question what sort of conduct in the face of danger deserves to be applauded. Rather he means that one must try to get insight into what it is that enables people to behave in the face of danger in the manner which we agree to call brave and which we agree deserves to be applauded. (I do not of course mean to imply that Plato had necessarily distinguished sharply between these questions). The definitions that he wants consist in insight into the nature of a thing, and he certainly says that questions about the thing cannot be settled until this insight is achieved, implying, probably, the converse that they can be settled once it is. If he got his definitions, then, he would use them to syllogize; if he could satisfy himself, for example, that moral goodness was some sort of knowledge, then he would conclude that it must necessarily be teachable. But the point is that in practice he does not ask his questions in the hope of getting satisfactory answers to them, but in the hope of *not* getting satisfactory answers. He exerts his dialectical ingenuity to pick holes in whatever answer anybody gives, even when the answer is one which, we suspect, he himself sympathizes with. In fact it is part of his purpose to show that neither he nor anybody else can give a satisfactory account of the nature of the realities for which even the most everyday concepts stand. At the end of the *Theaetetus* he more or less confesses that this is his purpose. If a man has an idea about something, it is always possible that it is a good one, in which case Socrates will play the intellectual midwife and help him to bring it to birth—help him to get the idea clear and to state it distinctly. But the

16

probability is that the idea is a bad one, in which case the midwife's function is to convince the mock-pregnant thinker of this, thereby rendering him "for the future a less tedious person". In the *Apology* (Plato's version of the speech made by Socrates at his trial) Socrates explains his destructive activities in the following way. A friend of his had asked the oracle at Delphi who was the wisest man in Greece, and the oracle had given this status to Socrates. Much puzzled by this (for he knew himself to be a fool) he had eventually come to the conclusion that the answer must be that while nobody knew anything, he alone knew that he knew nothing. He decided that the vocation to which Apollo was calling him was that of convincing men of the worthlessness of human wisdom.

Plato was the disciple of Socrates the intellectual midwife (or so he represents himself), and no account of Plato is satisfactory if it fails to stress that midwife's ruthlessness. One can of course speculate about the midwife's motives. In terms of the *Apology*, did Socrates imagine that Apollo wanted him to convince men that there *cannot* be human wisdom of any value, or merely that that which currently passed as wisdom was valueless? Was Socrates' vocation that of cutting down the brushwood of wild theories which choked intellectual growth, or was it that of persuading us that we cannot achieve wisdom from our own resources and must rely on divine guidance? Doubtless there was at least an element of the former in Plato's general outlook at all times, and certainly it was sometimes uppermost. Possibly the older Plato grew and the further he got from the influence of the actual Socrates, the more the desire for intellectual construction got the upper hand. Certainly when the Platonic Socrates emphasizes the importance of destruction he usually also allows the possibility of construction. Sometimes, for example in the *Republic*, he seems to believe that a very great deal of construction is in principle possible, though even there he makes it clear that almost superhuman efforts will be needed to allow it to occur. But on this type of question—on the question how much man can achieve by his own resources and how much must be left to good fortune and perhaps divine inspiration— Plato seems to have vacillated throughout his life. The *Republic* is an optimistic dialogue. It seems to allow that men can guarantee themselves a happy and virtuous life (though only if they take very drastic steps to ensure it); and this possibility seems to be denied (except for the very few) in the earlier dialogue *Phaedo* and in the later *Theaetetus*. Again the *Statesman*, from the last quarter, probably, of Plato's life, seems to tell us in a myth that nothing can go well in human affairs except under divine guidance. These passages are concerned, to be sure, with the organization of practical life, and, while Plato was fully aware that thinking is a practical activity, he might nevertheless have given it a better chance of succeeding than other practical activities; and certainly the *Statesman*, in the non-mythical parts of the dialogue, seems to assume that statesmanship is a feasible enterprise which could achieve anyhow a measure of success if gone about in the right way. If Socrates in the *Apology* means to suggest that no human intellectual achievements can be of any value, then it would be going too far to say that Plato consistently accepted this; but it would be going much too far in the other direction to say that he ever thought that wisdom was something which it is pretty easy to come by, or something which he had himself achieved.

But let us suppose that the midwife's motive in destroying was in the end constructive, that the brushwood of wild theories was to be got rid of to allow for intellectual growth. Does the brushwood consist simply in our propensity to believe that which we do not fully understand, or that for which we lack adequate grounds, or has it some more specific character? On this the *Phaedo* has something of interest to offer us. This dialogue purports to be an account of the conversation which Socrates had with his friends in prison on the day of his execution. The conversation is about immortality, and Socrates says that in order to settle as definitively as he can the question whether it is possible for a soul to die it will be necessary for him to give them an account of the development of his views on the nature of causal explanation, or in other words on the nature of that which determines what can and cannot happen. (To say that some causal explanation, E, is satisfactory is to say that E exhibits the phenomenon it is concerned with as an instance of a necessary connection; therefore the question "What constitutes a satisfactory explanation?" is closely related to the question "What necessary connections obtain?"). Socrates tells us that his faith was that mind determines all things and that therefore whatever happens does so because it is best that it should. This is interesting, but not to our immediate purpose. What is to our immediate purpose is the sketch that he gives of his attitude to the theories of his contemporaries on mathematical and scientific matters. For he seems to imply that it was a common characteristic of these theories that they were guilty of what we might almost call category-confusions, or at any rate inattention to differences of logical level. Mathematicians give account of mathematical operations like adding and dividing in terms of physical operations like cutting and putting alongside. Scientists consistently confuse a condition *sine qua non* with a cause—as one who explains why Socrates is sitting in prison by saying that his leg-joints are flexible (a *sine qua non* of sitting), rather than by saying that he does not think it right to try to escape. This leads to particularly unfortunate results in cosmology when cosmologists postulate imaginary whirlpools and other such mechanical devices to keep the stars in their courses, instead of trying to see what disposition of the heavenly bodies best commends itself to reason and must therefore obtain. Scientists in fact have been trying to go too fast and have obscured what they attempted to clarify by failing to keep things in their proper logical compartments.

Socrates does not make this point in so many words, but if he is indeed accusing his contemporaries of confusing logical levels, then the accusation would not be unjust. A good example of a pre-Socratic category-mistake is the Pythagorean attempt to maintain that things are literally made of numbers. Obviously reflection on the question what a number is makes it clear that, if "things are made of numbers" is meant for more than an epigram, it must be nonsense. What the Pythagoreans should have done, therefore, is not to wonder whether they could or could not get over the hurdle of incommensurables, but to ask themselves what a number is. Many other examples of category-mistakes can be found among the pre-Socratics—the soul treated as a kind of vapour, cosmic forces like "love" and "strife" put more or less on all fours with that upon which they are supposed to act; but for our purposes a particularly interesting category-mistake is one which Plato frequently illustrates in the earlier dialogues. Again and again Socrates is made to ask for the definition of some universal, for example,

beauty, and his friend is made to answer him by citing instances—
"That's easy, a pretty girl" as Hippias says in the *Hippias
Major* when Socrates asks him to define beauty. Therefore, if
the Pythagoreans had taken our advice and asked what a
number is, the likelihood is that the question would not have
seemed worth asking. "Surely it is obvious to everybody",
people would have said, "what a number is—6, 7, 8 and so on."
In other words people must be persuaded (and Socrates finds
great difficulty in persuading them) that the question what some
universal, P-hood, is cannot be answered by citing typical P
things; until they are so persuaded they cannot be induced to
carry out the sort of critical reflection which people must be
induced to carry out if they are to avoid the nonsense perpetrated by those who said that things are made of numbers.
We shall not get coherent accounts of anything until we succeed
in sorting our concepts onto different levels, and we shall not
persuade people to sort concepts so long as they think that one
can give a sufficient account of a concept by citing instances that
fall under it. Here, therefore, we have at least one purpose to
which Socrates' destructive midwifery was directed, namely to
destroy the habit of confounding a universal with its instances;
and we have seen that this might very well have been regarded
as essential preparation for the work of theory-building in all
fields, mathematical, scientific and philosophical in the
narrower sense.

We can say, then, that when we compare what we find in
Plato's writings with Aristotle's brief sketch of Platonism, the
destructive side of Socrates' midwifery is one of the things to
which the latter does not do justice. Two other things deserve
brief mention. Of these one is the obvious influence on Plato's
thought of Parmenides. Parmenides (an old man when Socrates
was a young one) had maintained a remarkable metaphysical
doctrine to the effect that the only thing that really exists is one
single homogeneous changeless sphere. Parmenides seems to
have arrived at this doctrine by realizing that there is no such
thing as nothing. There cannot, therefore, be either change or
plurality, for to explain the existence of either of these you must
illegitimately treat nothing as something. For change involves
movement, which involves empty space, or nothingness. Again

how can you have two things unless they are separated; and how can they be separated unless there is something between them; and what can this be except either some thing (in which case you have three things, about the diversity of any two of which the same question can be asked), or else nothing (which is to make nothing into an existent)? Possibly Parmenides was also influenced by the argument that reality must be one (for since it is everything there is, there can only be one of it); therefore existence must be unitary; therefore to exist must be to be unitary; therefore that which exists must be simple and undivided. Parmenides also maintained that there could be no false propositions, for a false proposition asserts what is not the case, and what is not the case is of course nothing. Holding these paradoxical opinions the Eleatics (i.e. Parmenides and his disciples) obviously came into conflict with common sense. They had to account for it and to counter-attack it. They accounted for it by according to it the status of opinion or seeming. The diverse and changeable world which seems to lie around us is somehow the way in which the single and changeless world of reality presents itself to us. They counter-attacked common sense by developing arguments which purported to show that the belief that the world consists of many substances is even more paradoxical than the belief that it consists of only one. In developing arguments of this kind Zeno and his colleagues did much to develop the practice of deductive argument. Indeed one of the roots of the science of logic is to be found in Eleatic disputation.

The influence of the Eleatics was considerable. It is probably to them that we ought to attribute the paternity of the notion that the reality of the world may be very different from its appearance, and that it is by rigorous *a priori* argument alone that we can ascertain the reality. Plato seems to have had his share of this Eleatic conviction, to the extent at any rate that he plainly does not think that things must be as they seem, and also to the extent that he feels it necessary to meet Eleatic arguments at their own *a priori* level. I see no reason to think that Plato was ever tempted to sympathize with Parmenides' conclusions, despite his respect for his methods. But he could not bring himself to dismiss Parmenidean monism, as he could dismiss, for example, the materialism of the man in the street or the wilder doctrines of the Heracliteans, simply by pointing out its unplausibility. What was presented as a deductively rigorous argument must be refuted with equal rigour; the doctrine that there can be no false propositions, though several times slightingly referred to (for example it is too subtle for Socrates' aged wits in the *Cratylus*), cannot be left alone until the logical error on which it rests has been precisely diagnosed. But at the same time I think it is fair to say that Plato learnt from the Eleatic movement to be deeply suspicious of the type of argument with which such unplausible conclusions could be demonstrated—that is of *a priori* arguments by which philosophically important conclusions are extracted by deductive methods from self-evident premises. He makes extremely little use of such arguments in his own work, and in the second half of the *Parmenides* he gives an exhibition of the facility with which whole hosts of contradictory conclusions can be arrived at in this way. He frequently insists on the importance in philosophy of looking through the words that we use to the realities about which we are talking; and he makes at times almost a parade of imprecision as if to remind the reader that the business of the philosopher is to use words suggestively so that the reader is brought to *see* what must be the case, not to attempt to compel his assent to something that seems to have the rigour of a mathematical theorem. Thus he concedes to Parmenides that there is of course no such thing as the non-existent, but he refuses to continue—"To say that a proposition is false is to say that it asserts the non-existent; but the non-existent does not exist and cannot therefore be asserted (for that which does not exist cannot have anything done to it); therefore to say that a proposition asserts the non-existent is to say of it something logically impossible; therefore we cannot sensibly say of any proposition that it is false." Rather when he discusses this topic in the *Sophist* he assumes that of course we can call propositions false, and of course can sometimes use "non-existent" as a predicate, and devotes his energies to discovering what we do mean when we do these things. It is a little difficult to decide whether Plato had the notion of a fallacious argument, that is to say whether he conceived of the existence of logical rules such that if we conform to them our deductive arguments will never lead us astray. If he did, then doubtless he held that the Eleatic arguments were fallacious; but in that case I think he would also have wanted to say that our ability to detect fallacious argument is insufficient to make it safe to rely on *a priori* reasoning of the Eleatic kind. Whether or not there are in theory rules which render such reasoning infallible, he seems to have felt that it is in practice treacherous. Like all of us he finds it difficult to resist the temptation to use an apparently cogent conceptual manoeuvre when it seems to guarantee a conclusion that he wants to arrive at, but in general he does not seem to put his trust in this procedure. The Eleatic tradition is essentially dogmatic, consisting in forcing one's assent to paradox; the destructive side of Socrates' midwifery is a resistance to all kinds of intellectual brow-beating, including this.

The other feature of Plato's thought, as we find it in the dialogues, to which Aristotle's account does less than justice is Plato's theism, or, perhaps it would be better to say, his belief in the cosmic efficacy of reason. Plato tells us in the twelfth book of the *Laws* that it makes all the difference to our attitude to the world whether we believe that consciousness comes into existence subsequently to the physical world, or that the physical world owes its order to the work of minds. The latter is of course, in his opinion, the right view.[1] A similar faith had, as we saw, been put into the mouth of Socrates, long ago, in the *Phaedo*. There can be no reasonable doubt that Anaxagoras' formula "Mind orders all things" to which Socrates there subscribes is absolutely central to Plato's thought. Whether he really believed in a transcendent personal deity as the creator of the physical universe is a somewhat tricky question. He certainly spoke not infrequently as if he did. The physical universe in the *Timaeus* is the "only-begotten son" of "a father and maker whom it is difficult to discover and impossible to proclaim to all men." But it is not impossible to treat such language as partly figurative. It may be that for Plato the creative reason was immanent in the world rather than transcendent and distinct. What is impossible is to doubt that for Plato the existence of an ordered physical universe containing definite and distinguishable things is due to the fact that the demands of reason are somehow

---

[1] This is perhaps the only important doctrine which Plato rests on an abstract argument of the Eleatic kind.

effective in it. If it is true that Plato believed in timeless essences for the reason that there had to exist entities which could be defined and known, it is at any rate equally true that a belief of this kind was a corollary of his belief in the eternal existence of reason and in its status as the orderer of the physical world.

Let us try to see the point of this discussion. The traditional account of Plato's thought, deriving ultimately from certain (rather cursory) passages in Aristotle, is along the following lines. The physical world is roughly what the Heracliteans said it was—a theatre of continuous change—and also roughly what the Parmenideans said it was—something which it is a natural delusion to believe in. The physical world is unreal, or only half-real; it consists of "becoming", not of "being". In a sense it is "there"; but what is "there" is something unstable, disorderly, inchoate. It is not an object of knowledge, not something which the mind can grasp. We cannot "know" it, nor, strictly speaking, know anything about it. We can have "beliefs" or "impressions" of it (for it affects our senses, and thus prints "impressions" on our minds), but we are ill-advised to treat these impressions as manifestations of reality. The physical world is the counterpart of one element in the human being, namely the body. That which stands over against the physical world, that which is the counterpart of the other element in man, the soul, that which is fully real and can be known is the world of "forms", essences or archetypes. These are eternal, changeless, intelligible, definable entities existing not in the physical but in the intelligible realm, and being as it were perfect non-physical exemplars of the things which exist in the physical world. It is by "participation" in the forms, or by some kind of striving to "resemble" these latter, that the contents of the physical world possess such definiteness and intelligibility as we can attribute to them. Interest in the physical world is an intellectual blind alley, just as concern with physical goods is a moral blind alley. The true end of life is the cultivation of the things of the spirit, and the true activity of the mind is the exploration of the intelligible realm of forms.

The important question is not the question whether Plato ever said things which lend themselves to this interpretation. It is undeniable that he did. It is undeniable that this account is at worst an unfriendly caricature of much that is to be found in his writings. The important question is the question whether such an account does justice to what Plato was trying to do, bearing in mind the conditions under which he had to work. Looked at in this light, this account of Plato's thought can be found inadequate on three important counts. Firstly it represents as static and dogmatic something that was essentially dynamic, critical, exploratory. Secondly it does less than justice to Plato's distrust—I say this deliberately, knowing that some will find it paradoxical—of dogmatic metaphysical constructions. Thirdly it does less than justice to Plato's belief in the cosmic efficacy of reason. I shall try in what follows to elucidate these criticisms.

We will begin by restating in a rather different form each of the criticisms we have just made of the traditional account of Plato's thought—of what we may call "Platonism" in inverted commas.

The first criticism was that "Platonism" renders static and dogmatic a body of philosophical work that was essentially dynamic, critical and exploratory. Roughly the same criticism can be made in rather different terms as follows.

Plato's position in the history of philosophy is that he stood at the very beginning of this intellectual discipline.[1] What may be called first-order philosophical theories—theories about the nature of reality and of our knowledge of it—had been advanced before his time. But there had been no critical reflection upon the nature of the concepts which are employed in such first-order philosophical theories. In consequence there existed no terminology in which one could draw distinctions which are familiar to all of us, such as that between the abstract and the concrete, or that between the objective and the subjective. Still less did there exist any terminology in which one could draw distinctions which are familiar, not to quite all of us, but to every student of philosophy, such as that between a concept and a property, or between a universal and a particular, or between what is false and what is non-existent. Nor was it just that there existed no terminology in which one could draw such

---

[1] Professor Havelock's *Preface to Plato* (a book I did not encounter until after I had finished this one) has some interesting things to say on this topic.

distinctions; also, as a not unnatural consequence of this, such distinctions tended to be blurred in thought. There were, in short, no words with which to draw the category-distinctions which are essential to a philosopher, and there was in consequence much confusion of categories. Now it would not be true to say that Plato did much towards developing such a terminology, but it would, in my judgment, be true to say that he laboured incessantly to get straight the distinctions which such a terminology is employed to mark. If he left the coinage of names for philosophical categories to Aristotle, nevertheless he struggled to distinguish some of the categories which Aristotle was to name. One might perhaps illustrate this by observing that, while Plato did not invent a word to stand for the concept of a universal, it is arguable all the same that he developed an idiom whereby he could unambiguously refer to particular universals, in contra-distinction to their instances. If he did not feel the need to invent language in which he could talk conveniently about universals in general, he did feel the need of a phrase whereby to make it unambiguously clear that he was talking about, say, beauty rather than beautiful things.

The relevance of this to our quarrel with "Platonism" as an adequate account of Plato's thought is as follows. Plato was trying, for much of the time, to invent logical shape. Much of his work, for example, is concerned with trying to bring out the distinction between an individual and a general term, much with trying to bring out that between what is non-existent and what is false. But in so far as he was trying to *invent* logical shape, there is a sense in which his thoughts could not already *have* logical shape. The effect of this is that there is (or it can be argued that there is) an essential fluidity about much of his writing; he is trying, often, to *bring out* what he cannot *state*. Therefore any account of what Plato meant, or of what he was trying to do, runs the risk of freezing into a set posture something which really consists of many postures; it is a bit like taking a still photograph of some manœuvre such as a dance. One has of course to admit that this criticism holds of *any* account of what Plato meant, including one's own. But one can also say this: if a man is going to try to give an account in post-Platonic language of the philosophical doctrine which he believes Plato was trying to communicate to his readers, then it must be a matter of judgment what account he is to give, and what language he is to employ in order to bring out what seems to be the significance of the intellectual manœuvres which Plato carried out. It is this which gives one some title to quarrel with Aristotle's account of Plato's thought to an extent to which one could not perhaps quarrel with, say, an account by Theophrastus of the thought of Aristotle. For Theophrastus would have used the same kind of language as Aristotle, whereas Aristotle did not use the same kind of language as Plato. Aristotle had technical terms where Plato had, at most, idioms. My contention is that Aristotle dissented indeed from the general direction of Plato's thought, particularly over the question of the relation between reason and the physical world; and that in consequence of this difference the account which he gave of Plato's thought, and the account which became in consequence traditional, freezes Plato's thought in one only of its postures, and, what is more, in one which is in certain important ways misleading as to the significance of Plato's intellectual activities. A legitimate difference of opinion between the two thinkers, taken in conjunction with Plato's position at the very source of second-order philosophical reflection, has led to some misinterpretation of Plato by Aristotle. "Platonism" in short does not do justice to the intellectual positions that Plato was trying to capture.

What these intellectual positions were can be brought out by considering our second and third objections to "Platonism". (They can, meanwhile be compendiously, or oracularly, expressed in a formula from the *Statesman*: "We know everything in a dream and nothing wideawake"). Our second and third objections to "Platonism" were that it does not do justice (*a*) to Plato's distrust of metaphysical structures and (*b*) to his belief in the cosmic efficacy of reason. I shall try to elucidate these criticisms by developing a line of interpretation which could indeed be justly accused of exaggerating certain features of Plato's thought, but features which it is, I think, salutary to exaggerate.

Almost Plato's only metaphysical certitude is that mind is something which is independent of the physical world, and yet responsible for the existence of the latter. This is his fundamental conviction, the one stability in his outlook; and everything else can be seen as an attempt at exploring what is involved in cleaving to this.

Mind is uncreated, eternal, self-existent, divine. It owes its activity to nothing but itself; it is self-activating activity. There are indeed derivative, created intelligences (we are ourselves examples of these), but they are the creations of intelligence. Since mind is independent of the physical world, and yet responsible for its existence as something ordered and determinate, it must be the case that the order and determinateness which are imposed upon the physical world are apprehensible by intelligence in themselves, and in abstraction from their embodiment in the physical world. Otherwise how could the creative reason have known, so to speak, what order it was going to impose before it had imposed it? If the order which was to be imposed was not in this manner known antecedently, then it must have been due to the features of that which it was imposed upon; and then in that case the physical world as an ordered system could not owe its existence entirely to the creative work of reason. Intelligence consists essentially in apprehending; and what is apprehended must be coeval with the apprehension of it. Therefore, if intelligence is independent of the physical world, the order which is embodied in the physical world must be independent also; it must exist in the manner in which intelligence exists, timelessly, spacelessly, owing nothing to the existence of the physical realm.

It is this which leads to Plato's conception of philosophical method, the conception which can be expressed in the image of birth, of bringing out into the daylight what already exists within. (The image of philosophy as midwifery is what we get to if we complicate this conception by adding to it the notion that thought is best done in collaboration with another). For we are ourselves intelligences. Since we are intelligences, we must possess the capacity possessed by the creative intelligence, namely the capacity of apprehending the principles of rational order, both abstractly and in their embodiment in things. We must be in principle capable of understanding everything. But a candid critic might be tempted to retort that in fact we understand nothing—or nothing perfectly. Yet this must not be taken too far. We do, after all, think; we employ concepts, even if we cannot analyse them; we can be taught to see necessary connections. If mathematics, for example, is a system of necessary connections, then it ought, one might have thought, to be an open book to us. It is not an open book, but equally it is not a book that we cannot begin to open. That we have the capacity to understand is the sign that we are intelligences; that this capacity is so largely unactualized must be the sign of something else.

This something else, this obstacle to the free play of human intelligence, is of course the physical order. On the side of the thinker it is what Plato calls the body; on the side of the object of thought it is the physicality of the things which, for the most part, we think about. What Plato demands can be illustrated, as he himself illustrated it, by considering the status of mathematics. For mathematics shows that the formal can be detached from the material. The lucidity of mathematics is due to the fact that the mathematician concerns himself with certain formal properties of things in abstraction from their material properties. He studies order in detachment from what is ordered. In the things which we encounter in the world we can separate out on the one hand the things with which experience familiarizes us and on the other hand the things which we can understand. We can be familiar with the taste of strawberries or the smell of pigs; we cannot understand them—for what would it be like to understand a taste or a smell? In so far as the notion of understanding applies at all to our knowledge of strawberries or pigs, we can understand them only as certain determinate forms of life. If you take the general idea of vegetable life, and specify it more narrowly by choosing between the various possible ways of implementing it (by deciding upon a certain manner of reproduction, a certain manner of growth and so on) you will eventually arrive at something which will, if you feed into it colour and taste and other sensible properties, give you the strawberry we are familiar with. The first or abstract part of this is the botanist's strawberry, the rest the consumer's. To the consumer the strawberry is, more or less, as Locke would have put it, a certain colour, a certain savour, and so on. It is because we are, as it were, consumers in our attitude to the world that we fail to understand it; if we want to understand it we must become like botanists. The philosopher is the man who, like the botanist, and still more like the mathematician, detaches the formal aspect of things from the material.

It may be retorted that it must be impossible, ultimately, to carry this programme through. The abstract, it may be said, is only arrived at by abstraction from the concrete. We cannot form a concept of man, for example, in any other way than by distilling what is common to a wide range of actual individual men. We must start from what is given in experience, and we never get away from this. But Plato would surely have objected that this line of argument makes reason in the end the product, and not the architect, of the physical world. If animals, for example, only exist because it seems good to reason that they should, then animality must be apprehensible independently of the existence of animals; it must be a timelessly given mode of existence, whether or not it has instances in space and time. It cannot be merely a concept which we form by isolating certain highly pervasive features of actual physical things.

It is in this light that we ought to think of the "theory of forms"—the theory that the concern of the philosopher is with the contemplation of timeless archetypal entities, rather than with the study of the physical world. It was never part of Plato's message that we should take no interest in the physical world. He does indeed demand that we should "withdraw" from it, in the sense that we should not be dominated by it; but this is not in order that we should ignore it, but that we should dominate it. It is the Aristotelian philosopher who retreats, when his duties permit, into the ivory tower of pure thought; the Platonic philosopher climbs towers not, or not only, to get away from the world, but to get a better view of it. When Plato tells us to think about, say, beauty itself, and not to attend to the many beautifuls, he is not telling us to ignore this world and attend to something which inhabits some other. Beauty itself is not remote from Helen of Troy and the Parthenon; it is the quality which, for a time, they had a share of. What Plato wants is not that we should lose interest in Helen and the Parthenon and think about something else called "beauty itself" instead. What he wants is that we should think about beauty, the quality they had a share of, but that we should not think of it *through* them, as it is embodied in them, but rather as it is in itself, independently of its embodiment in any individual embodiments. We have it in us, we must have it in us, to do this; for we are intelligences. If we fail to understand what we must be capable of understanding, namely what beauty is in itself, this must be because we insist on parochializing it, so to speak, by identifying it with the evident features of some set or sets of its instances. Instead of trying to understand the principle of organization which is responsible for the beauty of whatever is beautiful, we are content to familiarize ourselves with a selection of the concrete forms which that principle takes on when it is embodied in the more familiar kinds of material.

Beauty, equality, justice—we employ concepts such as these, and we must be capable of understanding the concepts we employ. It is in this sense that we know everything in a dream. That we cannot, nevertheless, give account of the concepts we employ is what is meant by the complementary truth that we know nothing wideawake. Philosophy is the process of trying to know things wideawake, the process of trying to understand what we are doing when we think. To begin to philosophize— to begin to dispel the dream—we must refuse to identify such entities as beauty or justice with the sets of things which, now and then, and in these and those relationships, manifest these properties. Justice must no longer be thought of as "telling the truth, paying one's debts, and doing other things of that kind". This is in my judgment the chief reason why at one period of his working life (roughly speaking towards the middle of his literary activity) Plato laid so much stress on the importance of attending to forms and ignoring physical things.

I have already conceded that there has been an element of exaggeration in these recent paragraphs, that I have concentrated the spotlight on that part of the stage that I want to direct the reader's attention to. I have said also that any account of the intellectual positions which Plato was trying to capture must be subject to the qualification that Plato doubtless could not have told us in advance what his objectives were, and that he was, perhaps to a greater extent than any subsequent philosopher, manœuvring in the dark, forging, to change the metaphor, the concepts that we have to employ in order to describe what we take him to have been doing. Having repeated these cautions I shall now try to fill out in further detail what I have so far only sketched in the roughest outline. In particular I shall try to tease apart the various strands of thought, the various intellectual battles, which seem to me to have led to the best known of Plato's philosophical positions, the so-called theory of forms. If in doing this I seem to make use of anachronistic distinctions such as Plato could not have drawn, to split hairs of whose existence he was unaware, I hope I have given a sufficient *apologia* for this.

3

"Platonism" and the Theory of Forms

IT is commonly said that Plato's metaphysical doctrine is the key to his whole philosophy; his opinions about morals, politics, art and so on are only intelligible in the light of his belief in essences or forms. Thus his reason for disapproving of representational art, it is said, is simply that artists do not depict essences and therefore inevitably operate on a somewhat debased level. All this seems to me to be fairly misleading. What is much nearer the truth is that the key to Plato's philosophy is his conception of the nature of philosophical activity. For this the image of the intellectual midwife is as illuminating as any other, and it is not for nothing that in one of Plato's best and most carefully constructed dialogues (the *Theaetetus*) Socrates is made to develop this image at considerable length.

When we think we employ concepts. If our thought genuinely applies to the world, then the world must exhibit features which our concepts correspond to. If *equality* for example is a useful concept then equality must be an objective relationship holding between things which are independent of our thought. Otherwise we shall find ourselves holding a pseudo-Kantian doctrine according to which the features of the only reality we can be acquainted with are bestowed upon it by the activity of thinking. About the relationship of some of our concepts to the world there is no problem. Redness for example is an obvious feature of many things, and the concept *red* is merely our recognition of this feature. Other concepts (*equality*, for example, or

33

beauty) are less easy to account for. Let us allow that equality and beauty are features of some of the things that the world contains; even so they are not features which the world obtrudes upon us in the obvious way in which it obtrudes sensible properties like redness. The former properties only attract the attention, so to speak, of those who are looking for them. We do not notice that things are equal unless we are comparing them; and to compare things is to look for equality or inequality. It is easy to imagine that a man might one day encounter a sensible property which he had never met before, and of which, therefore, his mind had no advance notice; indeed we all of us do this whenever we experience a new taste or a new smell. In the case of "intelligible" properties it is difficult to see how a man could ever encounter one which he was not already at least capable of looking for. When we discover that some animal can make use of such relationships as *being the same size as*, or *being a different shape from*, we tend to say that the animal has rudimentary intelligence, almost as if we thought that the ability to compare in point of size or shape was, and the ability to recognize colours or smells was not, something which intelligence has to contribute to experience, and cannot get from it. If we want to hold Locke's doctrine that the mind is a *tabula rasa* or blank sheet of paper at birth, and that everything that is in a man's mind has been written on that blank sheet by experience, then we shall find this easier to maintain in the case of sensible than in the case of intelligible properties. (Indeed Locke's *tabulae rasae* had to be endowed with powers of comparing, compounding and so on which we do not ordinarily attribute to blank sheets of paper). It is, in fact, tempting to suppose that in the building up of our understanding of the world there is an interaction between the mind and experience. Some of the features of the world we believe in are contributed by experience in the sense that the mind is pretty passive, to use Locke's word, in the reception of them; these are the sensible properties like redness or the smell of onions. Other features, however, those which are more abstract, more matters of structure than of content, are contributed by the mind, not of course in the sense that the mind somehow finds equality in objects between which this relationship does not hold, but in the sense that the mind has to seek it before it can find it. In that case, it

34

is at any rate tempting to say, we have to possess the concept of equality before we can find this relationship existing in the world.

We all of us have a considerable stock of concepts corresponding to intelligible properties. We can use the notions of equality and inequality, square and round, right and wrong, beautiful and ugly; we can count, measure, perform mathematical operations. Since we can use these concepts, we presumably have knowledge of the features of reality for which they stand. Yet if we are asked to give account of these features we stammer. We know and do not know what they are. We can say, and for the most part say with confidence, that these two objects are not equal in size or that such and such an action would not be right; yet we cannot give a lucid account of what rightness essentially is, and sometimes, when faced with a problematic instance, we cannot decide with confidence whether a certain action would be right or wrong. It is a little reminiscent of G. E. Moore maintaining that we know for certain that there are material things, but that it is highly dubious what the correct analysis of *material thing* may be.

The paradox that we know what we do not know runs through Plato's writings at all periods. In the *Meno* Meno is made to challenge the value of philosophical inquiry—of the search for definitions—by the argument that either we know the answer already or we shall not be able to recognize the right answer when we find it. Socrates is made to reply to this by allowing that philosophical discovery is always recognition, invoking the doctrine of reincarnation to explain how we can recognize that which is new to us: we have never previously understood it since birth, but we understood it before birth. He takes an uneducated slave and, by asking him the right questions, enables him to find the construction for a square twice the area of a given square. Socrates tells the slave nothing, and the demonstration therefore shows that the slave had it in him to find the right answers and to discover a necessary connection. He could not use this ability because he would not have been able, without Socrates' help, to take the problem step by step, asking the right question at the right time. He still does not understand what he has done, but, it is implied, if the right answers are elicited from him in the right order often enough, he will come to understand. He was able to give the right answers, Socrates argues, because he already knew what they were; and, since he had not learnt them on earth, he must have learnt them before he was born. Learning therefore is recollection. If we leave aside the reincarnationist element in this for a moment, we are left with the following. Everything is in one sense clear, but, since many things are also complicated, we are inclined to tie ourselves in knots. If, however, we are somehow saved from doing this, we can think correctly, and get the right answers without having to be told what they are. This is not in itself understanding or knowledge (but only correct opinion), but it can develop into understanding or knowledge if by frequent repetition, or some other way, we are enabled to see the necessity of what we have done. For knowledge involves "being able to work out the explanation".

Roughly the same point is repeated in the *Phaedo*. Here Socrates argues that we can use the concept of equality though we have not got it from experience—his explanation being once again that we must have got it before birth. But although we can use the concept of equality and do use it whenever we say in everyday life that two sticks are or are not equal, and also whenever we say in philosophic vein that no two physical things are ever perfect instances of equality, nevertheless we cannot give account of this relationship. We have the concept but we cannot give a satisfactory analysis of it. In both of these accounts the doctrine of reincarnation is invoked to explain how we know what we do not know, but I doubt whether Plato really believed that reincarnation was essential to the epistemological problem he is discussing. In the *Meno* Socrates explicitly makes the point that his argument shows that a mind must at all times, whether before or after birth, *have already* learnt everything that it can come to understand; therefore there never was a moment at which the learning occurred. It must be a timeless feature of the mind that to come to understand something is to elicit it from what is already in the mind.

In later dialogues doctrine of a similar kind is conveyed without the help of the doctrine of the soul's pre-existence. In the *Republic* Socrates compares that which he calls goodness to the sun. The point of the comparison is that while the sun is of course supremely visible, and is the source of the light in which we see everything else, nevertheless it dazzles us if we try to look at it; and in general anything that is better illuminated, and therefore more visible, than what we are used to (for example the outside world to one emerging from a cave) will be difficult and painful to the eyes. Similarly "goodness" provides the light with which all our thinking is done, but is itself the last thing that we can come to understand. We have to progress upwards from the intellectual cavern in which we normally live in comfortable reliance on our senses, accustoming ourselves step by step to each of a series of layers of more abstract entities or concepts, each of which is nearer to the source of intelligibility, and therefore at once "better lit" and also more "dazzling" to the mental eye than the one below it. Goodness, which is the source of intelligibility, is that which we can apprehend last, being hidden by the brightness of light. At the other end of the scale, the objects that occupy our attention down in the cavern are shadows of replicas of the objects outside in the sunlight. The shapes that we dimly discern are determined by those which are much too well lit for us to see them. We could not think at all, unless in the cavern-life of every day our thought was informed by some degree of apprehension of entities a proper apprehension of which is quite outside the reach of most of us.

The same point is made again and again, less vividly, in many of the short early dialogues where Socrates seeks and fails to find a definition of some ordinary moral concept, and concludes by exclaiming something like: "How strange that we three, who claim to be friends, can none of us say what a friend is!" (end of *Lysis*). It recurs in a late dialogue, the *Statesman*, where the Eleatic Stranger who leads the conversation says that nothing is intrinsically difficult; what is difficult is so because it is complicated. The elements into which the most complicated notions can in principle be spelt out are all familiar to us; and therefore we know everything in a dream and almost nothing in a wide-awake fashion. It seems to me that it is a most pervasive and essential notion in Plato's thought that everything that we can ever come to understand is composed of elements with which we are familiar, and correspondingly that we are all of us incapable of giving a satisfactory analysis of the concepts which we continually and, on the whole, efficiently employ.

This leads on immediately to the conception of the intellectual midwife. Philosophy is the activity of coming to an explicit grasp of what we possess implicitly. Essentially it is a co-operative process because no man is good at detecting the flaws in his own ideas. We tend to dote on our brain-children, and need another to show us their deformities. Philosophy, therefore, is dialectic or discriminative dialogue, with each man "refuting in friendly fashion" what the other says. Socrates the great mid-wife is himself sterile, being too old for child-bearing. This means perhaps that fecundity of ideas is characteristic of the young, both because they are capable of greater insight and also because they are more inclined to mistake bad ideas for good ones; they will get excited over what disillusioned age can see to be worthless. But philosophical conversation even between two young and fertile minds is or should be a kind of midwifery designed to elicit, each from the other, what is good in his ideas, and to get rid of what is bad. And what we are trying to do all the time is not to build up edifices of metaphysical deduction, but to understand properly what we already understand confusedly. "Dialectic" means, I believe, both dialogue and also a process of sorting,[1] and it consists in asking "what each thing is". That is to say it consists in taking some notion such as equality, number, justice, and asking how we use it, what we mean by it and, therefore, eventually, what is the nature of the entity, relationship, or whatever it may be, that the notion represents. We classify men and actions into just and unjust, and evidently there is some kind of principle in accordance with which we do it; but we cannot say what this principle is. The activity of the philosopher or dialectician is to ask relentlessly what it is, and to refuse to rest content with the assumption that we must understand it sufficiently since we use it, in practice, tolerably well. We do not understand it well enough even for practical purposes; without a proper theoretical grasp of what genuinely differentiates those we call just from those we call unjust we shall not be able to make decisions of principle in unfamiliar situations, nor shall we be able to differentiate things which may be superficially similar but substantially very different. Our situation will be worse still if we substitute, for the kind of rule-of-thumb discrimination of just from unjust which we picked up as children, a formula which purports to be an analysis of the nature of justice, but actually distorts it.

[1] EPD 2, pp. 562 sqq.

Nearly always the midwife has to destroy her client's brain-children, because he is better off without them. When, like Socrates, he knows that he is sure of nothing, he will be able to carry on his life by taking decisions which reflect common sense and the traditional wisdom; an unsatisfactory state of affairs, but one which is much better than that of being stuffed with theories that are either misleading in themselves or imperfectly understood, or both. Ignorance is the beginning of wisdom.

When a man tries to philosophize, what difficulties is he likely to encounter? One, discussed in the *Meno*, is intellectual paralysis. As Meno complains to Socrates, when you ask me what moral goodness is, and I try to tell you, and you show me that I am talking nonsense, I feel a little as if I have trodden on an electric eel; and can make no progress. The best we can do about this, Plato seems to suggest, is to suppose for the moment something that we do not know to be true, and see where this gets us. But of course it may get us nowhere, and we may have to resign ourselves to a condition of *aporia* or inability to progress, remembering all the time that having no answers is better than having bad ones.

But another and more particular difficulty that besets the Platonic Socrates in his incessant endeavour to pick pearls from his friends' brains is the inability of his friends to meet his questions on the level on which they are asked. "What a swarm of virtues!" Socrates exclaims when he asks Meno what virtue is, and Meno replies by listing the various forms which virtue takes in the various stations of life. What Socrates wanted, he says, is the one structure which must be possessed by all these virtues and which makes them all to be virtues. Again in the *Theaetetus* Socrates asks Theaetetus what knowledge is, and is given a handful of examples—mathematics, leatherworking and so on. "You generous fellow", says Socrates, "I asked you for one thing and you gave me many". Again and again when Socrates wants to know what something is (and he will consider no other questions about anything without first deciding what it is) he is not given what he wants, the one feature which is responsible for the X-hood of all X things; rather he is fobbed off with examples of X things, with features possessed by these and those but not by all sorts of X things, and other unacceptable substitutes. He is given many where he has asked for one.

D
39

"Platonism" and the Theory of Forms

To some extent this is a feature of the intellectual situation in which Socrates and Plato were working. Words for *thing, attribute, universal, instance, class, property, abstract, concrete,* had not been coined; beyond that, it seems that the distinctions which these words would have been used to mark had not yet been fully developed. Earlier thinkers used abstract notions, but they did not distinguish the abstract from the concrete. When asked to consider the abstract Socrates' victims do so in concrete terms. This is something we tend to consider a virtue; Plato evidently thought it a vice, and in his situation he was right to do so. It is one thing, in a culture in which abstract notions are current coin, to deplore discussions of, say, liberty which are not illustrated by concrete examples, nor put to the test of these. But it would be quite another thing to live in a cultural environment in which no conversation could ever maintain itself on an abstract level. Evidently Plato believed himself to live in such an environment, and thought it imperatively necessary to insist on the distinction between universals or essences and their instances or embodiments.

One reason why it was important to insist on this distinction can be found perhaps in the passage from the *Phaedo,* which we have already referred to, where Socrates tells us of his attitude to the problem of explanation. The student of nature wishes to discover necessary connections or universal concomitances. Scientific laws, and analogous truths in departments which we would not now call scientific, are in universal terms. You have not finally explained a phenomenon until you know what conditions obtain whenever and only whenever that phenomenon occurs. The pursuit of understanding commits us to the pursuit of necessary and sufficient conditions. It will not do, when asked what brings about some phenomenon, to reply by citing something that often but not always brings it about. The *explicans* and the *explicandum* must be co-extensive; or, to use language nearer to Socrates', it will not do to give as that which causes things to have some property P anything which is narrower than P-hood itself. Thus, to use one of Socrates' examples, it is relevant to the beauty of many beautiful objects that they are brightly coloured; to that of others that they are symmetrical. But one cannot say that it is their bright colouring, or their symmetry that makes these things beautiful. Or rather (to concede a point that Plato would not perhaps have conceded), one *can* say these things, and it may even be an apt diagnosis of an individual case to do so; but one cannot hold that saying such things involves insight into the nature of beauty, or of what in general makes things beautiful. In general nothing but beauty makes things beautiful. Trying to understand this topic, therefore, means trying to understand what beauty is, to analyse it into its components. In doing this it may perhaps be useful to collect together features such as symmetry or bright colouring which characterize sets of beautiful objects. This may be a useful preliminary step in trying to apprehend the nature of beauty (later on Plato was to lay some stress on "collection", by which he seems to have meant taking a synoptic survey of the various diverse species comprised in whatever one is considering); but it will not do to identify one or some of these features with beauty. If you do you inevitably get what Theaetetus gave Socrates—many in place of one. For if you say that bright colouring is beauty, then you will have equally good reason for conceding that symmetry is beauty; and so you get many beauties. What is beautiful is not always brightly coloured nor what is brightly coloured always beautiful. The way to resist the temptation to identify beauty with the prominent feature of some set of beautiful things is to remember (this point is probably made in the fifth book of the *Republic*) that there is none of the "many beauties" that one thus arrives at that is not also ugliness. That is to say, any characteristic that is not co-extensive with beauty must always be such that that characteristic can be present and beauty absent; indeed in the limiting case its opposite, ugliness, may be present instead. Nothing but beauty is that which makes things beautiful, and therefore an inquiry into what makes things beautiful is an inquiry into the nature of beauty. To list "many beauties", or diverse characteristics of sets of beautiful objects, may be a useful step in beginning this inquiry, but it must not be identified with it.

The part of this that is true has become so familiar and obvious that we tend to think Plato must have meant something more profound and more perverse. But the obvious has to be novel once. We tend also to concentrate on the part of this that is misleading. We say that Plato has no right to assume that beauty or knowledge or friendship is just one thing like, perhaps, diphtheria or magnetic attraction; and that half of Socrates' difficulties in finding satisfactory analyses of notions like knowledge come from this assumption that what he is trying to analyse is unitary. That the word "know" is not ambiguous, in the way in which "mine" is ambiguous, does not mean that there is something common to all cases of knowledge. Has not Wittgenstein shown that what makes all games games is not some essence which they all share, but a mere "family resemblance" which holds between them? No doubt this is a sound objection, though one may feel that it has been a little overworked of late. There is indeed some indication that Plato was himself aware of it in his later writings (for example the *Sophist* and *Philebus*) where he stresses how paradoxical it is that the one can comprehend the many and how difficult it may be to discern the comprehending unity. Partly perhaps he may mean, simply and misguidedly, that it is paradoxical that one property can have many instances; but I think he also partly means something a bit like Wittgenstein's "family resemblance" point—i.e. that in some cases that which unifies many diverse things (for example, their all being instances of knowledge) is not a simple common characteristic as it is in the case of, say, triangles (their having three sides).[1] But it is undeniable that in the earlier writings especially Plato tends too easily to assume that where there is a single non-ambiguous word in Greek, there must be some one thing that it stands for. *Sôphrosunê* is a good case in point. "Temperance" will usually translate this word, and it would be misleading to call it ambiguous, but it covers a rather wide range of traits of character. These may all be somehow connected with each other in such a way that none of them could appear at full strength without all the others, but it is dangerous to assume, as the *Charmides* perhaps assumes, that they must be connected in this way. However, it is natural to begin by assuming that a non-ambiguous descriptive word stands for some unitary common feature, to blame our obtuseness when we fail to find the feature in certain cases, and to wait until we have suffered a long run of disappointments before we conclude that the reason why we cannot find the feature is that it does not exist.

[1] EPD 2, p. 366; also p. 418.

But in the earlier writings at least Plato clearly thought that where we have some non-ambiguous descriptive word such as "knowledge", "beauty" or "friendship", there we must be using it to express some one concept, and that this concept in turn must correspond to some one feature which things do or might possess. He clearly believed also that it is because we possess some buried knowledge of this feature that we are able to differentiate the things which have the feature from those that lack it, and that it is important to exhume this buried knowledge (or to bring this infant to birth). He clearly believed also that one reason why we fail to do this is that instead of asking remorselessly what knowledge is we content ourselves instead with being able to list instances of it. We are content, in fact, with our ability to differentiate what has the feature from what lacks it, and will not trouble to try to understand the *rationale* of the differentiation. It is "evident to all men", we think, what knowledge is, and there we let it lie. But this means that we are content not to understand what we are doing. Familiarity with instances does not give insight into that of which they are instances. What is an instance of one general term is also an instance of many others, sometimes indeed of the contrary general term. What is in one comparison an instance of smallness is in another comparison an instance of bigness, what is double is also a half (4 is twice 2 and half 8), what is beautiful in one context may be ugly in another, what is right in one situation wrong in another. To be sure if we can produce a list of just actions we must have *some* knowledge of what justice is, even if we cannot analyse it; but that is what we start from, not what we are trying to get to. Whatever we can come to understand we already in some sense know. Philosophy is the activity of bringing to birth an explicit grasp of what we have always possessed implicitly. We could not philosophize if we could not use in everyday thinking the concepts which philosophy tries to classify, for philosophy in that case would have nothing to work upon.

To mark the difference between where we start from (familiarity with a general term in the concrete) and where we want to get to (explicit understanding of it in the abstract), Plato emphasizes in his earlier writings the difference between a general term such as beauty on the one hand, and on the other

43

hand its instances, or (what Plato does not carefully differentiate from these) the features such as bright colouring which are common to sets of its instances. There is a fact about the Greek language which did not help him in this. This is that it is common in Greek to express an abstract notion by a phrase consisting of an adjective or common noun, with, or sometimes without, the definite article. Thus one can ask what the beautiful is (meaning "What is beauty?") or what man, or the man, is (meaning "What is the essential nature of mankind?"). When this idiom is used no distinction is drawn between the property (beauty) and the class of things which have the property (the beautiful in the sense of that which is beautiful). It is thus natural for the man in the street, when asked what the beautiful is, to think first of the class and to reply by citing some of its prominent members or sets of these (Helen of Troy, or pretty girls and brightly coloured things). One has to labour, as Socrates labours with Hippias in the *Hippias Major*, to show the man in the street what is wanted. (Hippias' first answer to "What is the beautiful?" is "A pretty girl." When Socrates explains that he wants not an instance, but "that the presence of which to anything makes that thing beautiful" Hippias still thinks he is being asked a riddle, and conjectures that the answer to it is "Gold". For gold is surely pre-eminently that whose presence beautifies. Not only, in fact, does Hippias fail to see that he is being asked to analyse a property; it is also the case that Socrates has to hand no unambiguous language to make his purpose clear, and that the metaphor he does employ is readily misunderstood).

A philosophically more important example of this misunderstanding is provided by an argument by which, I suggested earlier, Parmenides may have been influenced. There is of course only one reality—that which is is one. We put this in the form "The existing is one." But these words might have been used to express the thought that existence is unity. By blending these meanings we move from the harmless thought that there is only one reality to the startling thought that reality is unitary.

In this transition there is a further linguistic feature (this time having no special connection with Greek) which we must notice. In "That which is is one" unity is an *attribute* of that which is; in "Existence is unity" unity and existence are *identified*. The verb which functions as copula may either predicate one thing of another or serve to identify what is on the left of it with what is on the right. It is no doubt perverse to take the identity-sense of the copula as primary; the predication-sense is much more common. But among Plato's contemporaries there were those who said that one could not say with strict truth that Jones is bald or that man is rational, on the ground that if these are construed as identifying being Jones with being bald or being human with being rational they turn into falsehoods. This is perhaps the kind of perversity for which the Eleatics were responsible. They had taken every opportunity of showing that ordinary discourse is philosophically misleading, and thus conditioned people to admit that strictly speaking so-and-so is of course false. Thus conditioned, one might be willing to admit that A cannot strictly speaking be B unless A and B are one and the same thing.

But if Jones is bald, then though Jones and baldness are not identical there is obviously some relation between them; if Jones *is* not baldness, at any rate he *has* it. To indicate the distinction between a general term and its instances it was necessary for Plato to coin special phrases to designate the former. "The beautiful" being ambiguous between the property and the class, phrases like "the beautiful itself" or "the thing itself which is beautiful" or "the beautiful itself according to itself" have to be invented to designate the property unambiguously. To indicate the relationship which obtains between a thing and its predicates, the relationship of *having* which holds between Jones and his baldness, and to make it clear that this relation is not one of identity, Plato made use of various metaphorical expressions. The predicate "was present to" the subject, the subject "had a share in" the predicate, or "was a partner in it"; the class as a whole was not, but "resembled", the property.

Phrases like these are certainly used as metaphorical designations of the subject-predicate relationship. They occur in contexts where any profound metaphysical implications would be out of place. It is possible that Plato may have inflated metaphors into metaphysics, but I see no clear indication in the dialogues that he did so in these cases. There is one place in the *Parmenides*[1] where Parmenides argues (in effect) that if S

---

[1] *Parmenides* 158, EPD 2, p. 341.

partakes in P then S must be capable of existing without P; for example, if men partake in animality, their animality must be something over and above their manhood in the way in which the meal I partake in is something distinct from me. But it is more likely that Plato is indicating the absurdity of this literal handling of the participation-metaphor than that he is himself deceived by it.

But at least in his earlier years Plato seems to have shared the assumption which led his contemporaries to say that Jones cannot strictly be bald, the assumption namely that "is" strictly signifies identity. We get the impression from many places that the beautiful itself is beautiful, and that this is true of nothing but the beautiful itself. I believe that language of this kind is explicable in terms of the assumption that "is" signifies identity; and that such language is primarily designed to enforce the distinction between talking about general terms and talking about their instances. To explain it we have to remember that the definite article is to some extent dispensable in Greek and that the indefinite article does not exist; we have to remember also that nobody had yet invented any terms for logical classification, grammatical classification, even, being in its infancy. In this situation "the beautiful is beautiful" is much the same as "beautiful is beautiful" and therefore much the same as "business is business". In that case how do you see that "the beautiful is beautiful" has the misleading implication that beauty is itself a beautiful thing? How do you see also that one can say "Helen is beautiful" without thereby misleadingly implying that Aspasia is not? For if Helen and the beautiful are one, Aspasia must be out in the cold. Plumbing can be *a* business, but it cannot be business, for in that case plastering, being not identical with plumbing, would not be business, nor a business either.

To put the point rather differently, it is a crude but natural theory of meaning to suppose that what a word means is identical with what it denotes.[1] The common noun "table", we might suppose, denotes tables, and these also fall within the

---

[1] Sometimes called the "Fido"–Fido Theory, because it holds, more or less, of proper names. *To denote* (as I am using the word here) is *to stand for*, in the way in which the name "Fido" stands for the dog Fido, and the word "table" stands for tables. A word denotes everything which satisfies its meaning.

denotation of "artefact", "wooden object" and so on. If you want to make it clear that what you are talking about is not tables, but that which they have in common, you will invent a phrase like "table itself" to indicate this. If you now ask yourself what "table itself" means, the answer must be that it means simply "that by virtue of which all tables are tables". This being what the word means, this is also what it denotes. But after all "table itself" is a phrase designed to refer to what "table" means. But if what a word means is identical with what it denotes, then the only thing that "table" can strictly denote is identical with that which is denoted by "table itself", namely that by virtue of which all tables are tables. This, one feels inclined to say, is no table, or anyhow no table made with human hands; and yet it must be not only a table, but the only table there is, because it is the only thing which perfectly fits the meaning of the word "table". What it is to be a table is the only thing that is without qualification what it is to be a table, and nothing else but that. This is, therefore, strictly speaking the only table, and everything else that is called by the word is a table only by courtesy.[1]

Now one might offer observations like this as, so to speak, a logical curiosity, or one might take them seriously as a basis for metaphysical theories. That is to say one might say things like "Table itself is the only real table" intending to make the point that nothing that we can encounter in the world perfectly and solely corresponds to the meaning of the concept *table* (for everything that exemplifies the concept (*a*) exemplifies it in one only of many possible specific forms, and (*b*) also exemplifies many other concepts); and one might make this point with a view to making the further point that we cannot treat the knowledge of a general term as the same thing as familiarity with its instances. Alternatively however one might say things like this with the metaphysical intention that over and above the courtesy-tables made with hands and met with in the world there is also in some transcendent realm just one real, unqualified, eternal table. One might indeed buttress this with the thought that, after all, the entities which we meet with in the world are no

---

[1] Compare the possibly rather similar worries about the relationship between subject and predicate felt by Lewis Carroll; see his *The Game of Logic*, p. 2, quoted by Geach, *Reference and Generality*, p. 115.

more than eddies in the Heraclitean flux, indefinable, unknowable, unworthy of serious consideration.

The entities we are talking about—table itself, the beautiful itself and so on—are the entities that Aristotle refers to as Platonic forms, and certainly at some stage between the germination of these notions in Plato's mind and Aristotle's account of them half a century or so later, forms had turned into transcendent particulars. Aristotle complains that the theory of forms explains nothing; for forms are merely what he calls eternal sensibles (i.e. eternalized versions of sensible things), so that the theory merely doubles the number of entities that has to be accounted for. A form then, by this stage, is not what we have represented it as being, a universal, a common nature, something which does or might characterize a particular. Rather it is itself a particular albeit a very peculiar one. The beautiful is not beauty, the characteristic shared by Aphrodite and Helen of Troy; rather it is something that can itself be said to be beautiful, as Aphrodite and Helen can, and beauty, of course, cannot. The table itself, likewise, it not the nature common to tables, but rather that which they aspire to be. If you take a table and subtract from it everything that is not part of the concept *table*—its woodenness, its beauty or ugliness, its having been made by somebody, and so on—and if you suppose that what you have left after performing this subtraction is something that can still be called a table, then this sort of entity is what a Platonic form is in Aristotle's account of it.

It is not clear what is to be made of this. One possibility is that Aristotle's account does full justice to Plato's best thoughts. Another is that it does justice to rather tired things said on this topic in the Academy by Plato himself, perhaps, or by his disciples. Yet another possibility is that Aristotle did not mean to tell us that Plato *actually* thought that table itself was a transcendent, eternal, not-wooden, not-manufactured table, but that this was what Plato *ought* to have thought. Table itself, on this view, was what we have taken it to be—tabularity or the nature common to tables; but Plato maintained that tabularity was something real, indeed more real, if that makes any sense, than actual tables. But that which exists, for Aristotle, is primarily individual substances; whatever else exists is ontologically dependent on these. Therefore, in making tabularity or beauty into

48

primary existents Plato was, or should have been, making them into individual substances; and what sort of individual substance could tabularity be but an "eternal sensible", a dephysicalized version of an ordinary table?

Which is the more incredible—that Plato should have actually believed in the existence of an individual eternal substance which was just exactly what "table" means, or that Aristotle, exasperated perhaps by formulas unthinkingly repeated in the Academy, should have judged that nonsense of this kind was fair comment on what the utterers of these formulas were committing themselves to in the light of his own beliefs about the nature of things? (In either case we may assume that Plato will have used language which *could* be taken to imply the existence of "eternal sensibles"). I leave the reader to make his choice. Meanwhile let us ask whether we find in the dialogues any clear traces of the theory of forms as Aristotle describes it— the theory, that is, that for every set of mundane things there exists in an eternal realm just one intelligible entity which is exactly what one of these mundane things would be if one subtracted from it firstly everything that makes it mundane and secondly (I think) everything that makes it satisfy any description other than that description under which we are currently considering it. (Thus the beautiful must be a beautiful thing, but a thing that is nothing whatsoever except beautiful).

To be dogmatic, there are no clear traces, but many ambiguous indications. These latter may be divided into two kinds. One of these consists of the places where Plato says or implies that P-hood, or the P itself, can be said to be truly P, and is the only thing of which this can strictly be said. For this naturally seems to imply that the beautiful is an individual substance having just one attribute, namely beauty. But we have seen, I hope, that such language may have been rather forced upon Plato by incoherent theories of meaning than designed to imply this, or indeed anything else. His purpose, I have suggested, may have been to safeguard the distinction between a general term and its instances, and such language may have been forced upon him in the light of this purpose by the fact that ". . . is P" could be taken to be ambiguous between ". . . has P-hood as an attribute" and ". . . is identical with P-hood." To

49

guard against this ambiguity, he might have felt, let us use ". . . is P" only of P-hood itself, preferring the formula ". . . partakes in the P" for its instances.

The other kind of ambiguous indications consists of numerous places where Plato uses about the forms language which must, on the view that forms are not transcendent individual substances, be described as rather picturesque. For example in the *Phaedrus*, in a mythological presentation of the doctrine of recollection in terms of reincarnation, discarnate souls are shown processing round the heavens in the wake of the gods, looking upon the forms; and it is this pre-natal vision of the forms which enables us subsequently to recognize their instances. Picturesque language of this kind is not intrinsically troublesome. Plato is a picturesque writer, continually dramatizing, personifying, preferring metaphor and simile to plain statement. More formidable are passages like that in the tenth book of the *Republic* where Plato speaks of three beds, one which a painter makes when he paints a picture of a bed, one which a carpenter makes when he manufactures a bed, and one which God makes and the carpenter copies, this last being the only one which is really a bed. This may seem a nut too tough to crack by facile remarks about Plato's habit of picturesque writing. But we can crack it by other means. For in this very passage Plato observes that bed itself, which God makes, is something which is by nature one. God could not have made two specimens of bed itself; had he done so, they would have shared a common nature, and it is this, and not they, which would have been bed itself. But what does this mean if it does not mean that "X itself" denotes that which is by nature one because it is that which two or more instances of some universal have in common—in other words the universal or common nature which they share?

I must repeat at this point that the notion of a universal or common nature had not yet been isolated, and Plato's earlier writings about entities like the beautiful itself are the process by which it was isolated. It would be absurd of course to suppose that Plato knew what he was doing before he had done it. I cannot truly say "I am going to invent the concept C"; if that can be said at all, C has already been invented. Doubtless, therefore, there was much obscurity and groping in Plato's mind while he was trying to play the midwife to the notion of a common nature. But what does seem to be from our point of view clear is that when Plato speaks of entities like "the P itself" what he has in mind is something like the nature P-hood. Where P is an artefact such as a bed this seems to amount to the intelligible principle in accordance with which a well-designed bed would be constructed; and the same is probably true of a work of nature rather than of man. The animal itself, therefore, will be more or less the general design of a living creature, that which has to be conformed to by anything which is to live and move about. When the P itself is something which is already abstract like the similar itself or the square itself the position is slightly different; the similar itself is similarity, and the square itself is squareness, or rather, as we shall see later, it is that which is "intelligible" in these entities.

Whatever A and B may be, if we can talk of A and B, then we can refer to them—by using, for example, the pronoun "them". We can speak of Jones's habit of wrinkling his nose, and refer to it as "it". If Jones does wrinkle his nose, then we shall have to say that it exists; and perhaps it is irritating, or amusing. We must in other words use about entities such as this language which suggests that they are individual substances. Anything that can be talked about can become a logical subject and thus masquerade as a thing. Whoever talks about abstract entities must therefore make them masquerade as things. Plato may well have been deceived by this, at one time, or at all times, and have supposed that forms must be some kind of transcendent substances; again he may well not have been deceived but merely have used language giving that impression. The only place where Plato himself discusses this matter is the *Parmenides*, and perhaps the only conclusion which can be quite safely drawn from this dialogue is that Plato was aware of the problem. In the first part of this dialogue Socrates (as a very young man) argues that it is not surprising that Zeno can demonstrate that particular things have contradictory attributes; for particular things are not identical with, but merely partake in, forms or attributes and, therefore, presumably, can partake in both of two contradictory attributes without thereby identifying the latter. (S can partake both in P and in not-P without damaging the distinction between P and not-P; this would not be the case if S were identical both with P and not-P).

But Socrates contends that it is incredible that anybody should demonstrate that forms can enter into incompatible relationships not only, as he puts it, in things (as when S partakes both in P and in not-P), but among themselves. The P itself, in fact, cannot be not-P. Whatever exactly Socrates means by this, Parmenides seizes on Socrates' assumption that there are such things as forms and that the relation of particulars to them is that of participation, commends it, but demands an analysis of participation. Socrates fails to supply one which can stand up to Parmenides' criticisms. It seems to me that two conclusions follow from their argument. One is that "participation" cannot be taken literally; we cannot suppose that beauty is parcelled out among beautiful things. The other is that the relationship of a particular to a form cannot be one of similarity; for if it were the form would be one of its own particulars. The implication of this is of course that a form is that in point of which a set of similar particulars are similar.

So far as it goes this tends to show that forms cannot be treated as things, certainly not as perfect transcendent exemplars of their instances. This conclusion seems to me to be reinforced in the second part of the dialogue where Parmenides is made to discuss the proposition *that the one exists* and to show that, whether this proposition is asserted or denied, the one can be shown to have each of more or less every pair of incompatible predicates. This incidentally shows that antinomies can be demonstrated, on certain conditions, about anything. However the main upshot of the argument is, I think, to discredit the assumption which, we thought, had tempted Plato to say that strictly only the beautiful is beautiful, and other things of this kind, the assumption namely that the meaning and the denotation of a term are identical, or that the only thing which satisfies the meaning of a term is the meaning itself. For the discussion seems to show both that one cannot deny that there is such a thing as unity (for everything that exists is one thing), and also that one cannot assert that unity is unitary except in the sense in which anything is unitary (Greater London, for example, for it is *one* conurbation). That which "unity" designates (to wit unity) is something complex; if unity exists, it cannot be "just what unity is", or in other words that it is unity cannot be all that is true of it. For whatever exists is complex, being at least itself and also an existent. Perhaps what Plato was chiefly trying to bring out by this argument is as follows. He had tended to assume that statements of the form *S is P* (i.e. statements where a predicate is predicated of some subject other than itself—e.g. "Jones is wise") can only be made where the subject is a particular. In the case of a general term such as unity or wisdom nothing can be predicated of it but itself. He now sees that this is incorrect, and shows this by arguing that one is forced to admit in the case of unity not only that it is an existent, but even that it is, therefore, paradoxically enough, in a sense complex. That attributes themselves have attributes is a point to which Plato attached a good deal of importance in his later dialogues. But the argument is probably also intended to show, not that an attribute cannot have itself as one of its own attributes (which is not perhaps in general true), but rather that no existing thing can ever have just one attribute (for it must (*a*) exist, and (*b*) be differentiated from other existents), and that it cannot therefore strictly be the case that an attribute is its own unique and perfect exemplar in the sense that the attribute alone is just itself and nothing else. (It is of course itself and nothing else in the identity-sense of "is", but in the predication-sense this is not true). This opens the way to seeing that a word or concept can perfectly well have application without there having to exist entities, or an entity, which simply embodies the concept and nothing else. "Table" applies to tables, i.e. to things which are wooden, manufactured, beer-stained and many other things not entailed by the concept of table. Table itself, therefore, is not the only thing that can be strictly called a table. Indeed it cannot be so called.

All this seems to me to be part of what is involved in bringing to birth the notion of a universal or common nature, in getting clear about the logical relationship of "beauty" and "beautiful thing". It is difficult to decide whether Plato is extricating himself from a mistaken doctrine that he had subscribed to, or seeing how to avoid a misleading way of talking. Is it that he has come penitently to see that forms are not perfect particulars, that beauty is not a timeless beautiful thing, but rather the principle conformity to which confers beauty on whatever has it? Or is it rather that he has come to see that that which a word applies to is not identical with what it means, with the result that we do not have to say, even strictly speaking, that only the beautiful is beautiful? On the whole I think the latter view is correct, but the question is not perhaps very important, because in either case we can say that the general tendency of Plato's thought is towards clarifying the distinction of logical level which holds between universals, attributes or common natures on the one hand and their instances on the other. This is what he is trying to do, whether or not he is doing it over his own dead body.

(At this point we may interpolate something which arises now, but which we shall not make use of until later. When Plato came to see that "Helen is beautiful" is correct in logical form, whereas "Beauty is beautiful" is incorrect, he would not necessarily have felt enthusiastic about saying that statements of the first pattern can often be safely assented to without qualification. Many statements are correct in logical form without being true; and some statements that are true are misleading. Now "Helen is beautiful" would have seemed to Plato misleading, at best, if it was taken to mean that beauty was *manifest* in Helen, or that one could come to see what beauty was by taking Helen as a sort of ostensive instance of it, in the way in which a pillar-box may be an ostensive instance of "scarlet"—something that can be pointed to as a manifestation of the whole meaning of the word. With certain reservations it can be said that a sensible quality like a colour is present in its entirety in each of its instances. There is nothing to scarlet, so to speak, over and above its being the colour of, for example, pillar-boxes. He who knows what things are scarlet knows what "scarlet" means. But he who knows what things are instances of beauty does not necessarily know adequately what "beauty" means. Beauty is not present in its entirety in each of its instances; or at least, if it is present, the manner of its presence is not such that the nature of the quality can be adequately grasped by one who knows that this and this and this are a representative set of its instances. There is not present in Helen the beauty of a beautiful character, nor of a beautiful poem, but only the beauty of a beautiful woman; and even this has not been present at all times when she has been Helen, and is not always apparent, even today, when she is admittedly a beautiful woman. It is not apparent, for example, when she is feeling sea-sick, or when she is placed in some setting in which her *soignée* appearance is inappropriate. To see Helen's beauty—to apprehend what it is that makes it right to say that she is a beautiful woman—we must find embodied in her, sometimes, and in some settings, that which we can also find embodied in a beautiful poem or a beautiful demonstration in mathematics. "Helen is beautiful", therefore, is the sort of remark which must be accepted only guardedly. It is, so to speak, fair comment on Helen, but it is not the low-down on beauty. And statements of the form *S is P* do have these two uses—"Pillar-boxes are scarlet" may be meant to convey information about pillar-boxes, or about the colour scarlet. Considerations like these might have restrained Plato from agreeing with enthusiasm that Helen is without qualification beautiful even after he had ceased to think that only beauty could with strict propriety be said to be beautiful. This, however, is for the moment a digression from our main argument).

The general drift then of the (not very numerous) passages in the earlier dialogues where Plato talks about forms is to extricate and clarify the notion of abstract entities such as universals. But this means, surely, that forms are not among the things that primarily exist. For abstract entities only exist in so far as they are embodied by concrete entities. There can be no measles without patients to suffer this condition, nor circularity where there are no physical things to have this shape. Either, therefore, Plato's forms must have been what Aristotle says they were—eternal sensibles—or he must have admitted that they existed only in their embodiments. But notoriously Plato admitted nothing of the kind. Forms were unquestionably real and in no sense owed their existence to their embodiments; indeed it has been argued that Plato thought they had no real embodiments, tables striving, but failing, to be true instances of tabularity. Surely then forms must have been eternal sensibles.

But this argument entirely misconceives Plato's reasons for maintaining the reality of forms and their independence of their embodiments. There are two very different motives intertwined in all this. So far we have discussed the relationship between orms and particulars in terms of the philosophical tangles that a man will get into if he fails to keep his logical levels distinct. That was one of Plato's motives for insisting on the distinction. But this motive fails to account for one important feature of Plato's treatment of forms, namely the fact that one can intelligibly ask the question whether there is a form of so-and-so —man, fire, mud, hair and dirt. Parmenides puts this question to Socrates, and Socrates hesitates over the first two and answers "No" to the others. But why can one intelligibly ask whether there is a form of man? (One cannot intelligibly ask whether men share a common nature—of course they do). The answer to this question answers the objection stated in the previous paragraph. Forms are abstract entities such as universals, but not all abstract entities are forms. There is indeed distinction of logical level between abstract entities and their embodiments, but that does not of itself entitle one to say that abstract entities exist other than in their embodiments. There would be no muddishness if there were no mud. The reason why the existence of some abstract entities is independent of their embodiments (if they have any), is that to do away with these entities is to do away with intelligence. The objection in the previous paragraph, Plato would have argued, is the objection of a man suffering from the fundamental intellectual delusion, the delusion that mind is a product of matter.

Both Plato and Aristotle took for granted that mind is not a sort of machine. Mind is nothing but receptivity—the capacity of an intelligent being to apprehend order and structure. We tend to think of mind as a probing instrument or searchlight; the Greeks tended to think of it as a kind of wax or blotting paper. Therefore, mind and its objects are strict correlatives; there can be no intelligence without intelligible principles. Just as there can be no smelling without smells, and yet the smells do not exist in the smelling but are independent of it (it being the receptivity and they what is received), so if there is reason there are the rational principles which it apprehends, and these are independent of it. If, therefore, you make all abstract entities such as circularity depend for their existence on the existence of circular physical things, then you make intelligence coeval with the existence of the ordered physical world. But in that case mind can hardly be responsible for the order of the physical world.

Aristotle of course disputed this. Aristotle's God was coeval with the physical world, and the two were on the same ontological level. Perhaps Aristotle was right in this, but Plato would not have agreed with him. To Plato, whether or not the ordered world had a beginning in time, at least it owed its order to the creative intelligence, which was in no sense dependent upon it nor bound up with it. Therefore, that which intelligence is the apprehension of must also be independent of the ordered world. This means that there must be some entities of an abstract or intelligible kind which are independent of the ordered world. It means also that not all abstract entities need enjoy this status. The forms are those which must.

That the forms are those entities which must be independent of the physical world, if intelligence is to be independent of it, led Plato into many subtle speculations. He seems to have striven continually to dissect entities like circularity into a formal element, so to speak, and a material—into an element which is independent of spatial extension and therefore correlative with the intelligence which is independent of the extended world, and an element which is not independent. As early as the *Republic* we find him implying that mathematics is a sort of half-way house between forms and their concrete instances. The word "square" commemorates the observation that there is a certain identity of structure between a rectangle whose two dimensions are identical and a number which is a product of some factor by itself. The Pythagoreans had extended the identity of structure from squares in geometry and arithmetic to reciprocity or justice, the situation in which reward equals merit. The same principle, so to speak, can be expressed in geometrical figures, numbers and human transactions. Plato seems to have taken this seriously, and to have drawn the conclusion that, if this is so, then it is the principle thus expressed which is truly the form, its mathematical expression being no more than a particularly clear "image" of it.

A similar motive seems to have been behind the philosophy of mathematics which Plato propounded in the Academy. We know of this only from Aristotle's hostile account of it, and this gives us little to draw on. But it seems clear that Plato tried to derive the fundamental entities of arithmetic from others such as unity and multiplicity which are of the highest generality, and to derive the fundamental entities of geometry from numbers and space.

But the most interesting of Plato's attempts to dissect general terms into a formal and a material element is to be found in the *Philebus*. Here Plato suggests that entities such as health, which play a part in the orderliness of things, can be regarded as functions of what he calls the definite and the indefinite. The definite is the organization, the indefinite that which is organized. The organization, he implies, is, if not exactly a matter of number, at any rate quasi-numerical. The indefinite he characterizes as "that which can be more or less", temperature and moisture being examples of it. The indefinite in fact is a parameter or respect in which things can be compared. Disorderly states of affairs such as disease are to be understood in terms of the indefinite alone. The point of this is that whereas there is such a thing as health, and it obtains when some one definite relationship holds between the bodily elements, there is not correspondingly any such thing as disease, but only an indefinite variety of deviations from the norm. The reason for this is that the natural world is essentially unstable and will not persist in any pattern except it is constrained to do so. Constraint upon the instability of the natural world is exercised only by intelligence, which is of course concerned to produce order, not disorder. The only persistent patterns, therefore, which recur in nature are those which constitute its orderliness. In some individual case of disorder, such as the disease from which Jones is now suffering, there is of course some determinate relationship between the values of the variables involved—temperature, moisture and so on. But there is no one determinate relationship characteristic of disease, as there is in the case of health; and therefore while health is a function of the definite and the indefinite, disease is to be thought of simply in terms of the indefinite.

(Abstract entities, therefore, can be classified into those like triangularity which are definite attributes, those like temperature which are ranges within which things vary, those like health which arise when an orderly pattern obtains between these variables, and those like disease which consist in deviations from this norm. It is still possible to read contemporary discussions of universals which treat colour, for example, as an attribute which is more generic than that of being red. Reflection upon the *Philebus* might suggest that it is better to treat colour as a range, and redness a determinate position within it).

It is difficult to decide whether Plato would have wanted to regard certain examples of the first item on the list (structures, such as triangularity) as forms or whether he would have given this title to the third item (functions of structure upon a range of variation, such as health). Is a form the formal element within a general term such as health, or is it the general term as a whole? It is likely that two opposing considerations would have made this question a difficult one for Plato to answer. He seems to have wanted forms to be totally independent of the existence of the world of space and time, so that circular shape is not a form but an image of a form, an expression of it in terms of space; this would tend to identify the form with the formal element in a general term. But he seems also to have wanted a form to be that of which intelligence produces instances when it brings order out of chaos; and this would have tended to identify the form with the general term as a whole. To the one way of thinking the form of health would have been a certain ratio or structure which does hold between the variables of an animal's constitution but which may well hold between other elements. To the other way of thinking health would have been that structure holding between those variables.

It is not possible to ask further which way of talking Plato would have preferred; there is not enough evidence. We can sum up our recent discussion, however, in the following propositions. (1) A form is an abstract entity, a nature, structure or principle which many things may, logically, exhibit or conform to. (2) A form is independent of the existence of physical instances of it, since forms are what reason apprehends, and reason is independent of the physical world. (3) Not every abstract entity is a form, those in which reason is not interested— for example sense-properties such as colours—lacking this status. (4) It is possible to dissect the kind of abstract entity which is qualified to be or to have a form into a formal and a material element; whether the form is to be identified with the first of these or with both taken together is not clear. (5) When Plato is talking about the difference in logical status between general terms and their instances, he is not always concerned with the question whether the general terms he is discussing have the status of forms. (For example in the fifth book of the *Republic* Socrates says that ugliness, like beauty, is one thing and not many. It does not follow that Plato would have wanted to call ugliness a form. Logically "ugliness" is a universal-word, but that which it stands for is probably an indefinite variety of deviations from a norm).

Indeed I think this last proposition could be strengthened. It seems to me that when Plato speaks of entities such as the P itself in the dialogues it is seldom the case that he is particularly interested in the question what ontological status he would want to accord to the entity that he is talking about. He is more concerned to insist that a general term cannot be satisfactorily discussed in terms of its instances. It may be that his state of mind was such that if you put to him the question: "Do you think that beauty and ugliness are on the same level?" the proper answer for him to give would have been: "Logically and epistemologically, yes; ontologically, no. That is to say 'ugliness' is the same sort of expression as 'beauty', and one can no more delineate the nature of ugliness by stringing together instances of it than one can do this in the case of beauty. Since, however, ugliness is simply the privation of beauty, the two entities have not the same status." It may be that if you had asked him whether beauty and bed-hood had the same status the proper answer would have been: "Logically and epistemologically similar; ontologically different." It may be also, of course, that, lacking convenient verbal tools such as "ontologically", he would not actually have given these answers. But from the suspicion that he would not have said: ". . ., ontologically different" we are not entitled to infer that he would have said ". . ., ontologically the same." Whether he would or not is a question we must judge on its merits, in the light of what he seems to be trying to do.

4

The Physical World

THERE are places in the dialogues where Plato's language seems to imply that there are no instances in the physical world of entities such as beauty or equality, but only approximate instances, and that we cannot discover in the physical world the sharpness of definition which obtains in the realm of the intellect. At the abstract level hardness and softness are opposites and quite incompatible with each other; at the concrete level the same thing can be both hard and soft.

That the physical world is, from the point of view of reason, a pretty disreputable place is an attitude that Plato might have got from his youthful indoctrination into Heraclitus' belief in universal instability, from Parmenides' contrast between the way of knowledge and the way of opinion, and from the Orphic-Pythagorean view that the interests of the soul are in conflict with those of the body. It is clear that he had this attitude fairly strongly in his youth and that he still paid it lip-service occasionally in his old age, but it is also clear to me that his explicit beliefs were never fully in conformity with it, and diverged from it increasingly as time went on. This is not at all an uncommon situation; people tend to profess the political allegiances they formed in youth long after they have ceased to think and act appropriately.

How do we account for the impression Plato sometimes gives us that the physical world is an incoherent place, incapable of embodying rational principles or forms no matter how hard reason tries to impose them upon it? Part of it can be accounted for, as we have already seen, by supposing that Plato thought, not that no action can ever be perfectly just, but that no action can ever be identical with the just. So long as he supposed that "This act is without qualification just" meant, strictly speaking, "This act and the just are one and the same thing", he would be obliged to hold that this remark is strictly speaking false. It is only if Plato said somewhere that no act ever partakes perfectly in the just that we could conclude that he held that there were never any instances of just action in the world. So far as I know he never does say things quite like this. If, however, there are such places, we have seen above one train of thought that might account for their presence, as it will also help to account for the passages (which we certainly do find) where Plato says that whatever has some quality also lacks it. This was the consideration that, since Helen does not luminously and fully body beauty forth, there is something insalubrious about the form of words "Helen is beautiful." For if we take this in the spirit of one who takes the statement that pillar-boxes are scarlet to be telling him what colour scarlet is, then it is grossly misleading. Not only is it the case that Helen is not identical with beauty; it is also the case that beauty is not identical with what Helen manifests, that "beautiful" and "Helen-like" do not mean the same. This might have seemed a reason—a rather incoherent reason, certainly, but still a reason—for refusing to allow without qualification that Helen, or even Aphrodite, is beautiful.

There are certain places, as we have just observed, where Plato says that whatever can be called (e.g.) just can also be called unjust; and this certainly tempts one (and may perhaps have tempted Plato) to believe that Plato thought that the world we live in is a hazy and indeterminate place. But I do not believe that this is what he is really trying to say. It can be argued with truth that such remarks occur (in the *Phaedo* and in the *Republic*) in passages where his chief purpose is to argue that you cannot acquire insight into the nature of something like justice from scanning its instances. The argument is that if you take any action such as paying a debt which would be in most contexts just, still you can always find a context in which it would be unjust. Therefore, if you identify "the just" or justice with "the many justs" (paying debts, telling the truth, punishing crimes and so on) your conception of the just will include a proportion of the unjust. Thus "Whatever is just is also unjust" is to be understood as cautioning us, not against supposing that a just act can ever be done, but against supposing that justice can be defined by summing up the descriptions ("debt-paying", etc.) under which just acts tend to fall.[1]

Other passages can be dealt with as follows. When Plato complains of "the world revealed by sight", telling us that the hard things in it are also soft and so on, there is an ambiguity we must be wary of. The world revealed by sight may be the actual world that we literally see when we open our eyes. On the other hand Plato sometimes takes sight, in a metaphorical way, as a representative of common sense, so that "the world revealed by sight" will mean the world as common sense conceives of it. When he says, therefore, that what the senses class as hard they can also in a suitable context be induced to class as soft, the complaint may be not one about the inconstant constitution of physical things, but about the unthinking way in which the man who relies on "sight" (or in other words on the senses, without critical reflection upon them) allots such predicates as "hard" and "soft". Being an indefinite notion "hard" is always elliptical; when the ellipse is supplied ("harder than when ripe" for example) all is clear. Since we do not normally bother to think what standard we are comparing something with when we call it hard, we sometimes find ourselves calling the same thing hard and soft. If we suppose, as we tend to do, that the senses give us an adequate picture of the world (i.e. that the world is just as we talk of it when we report our observations uncritically), then we shall think that the world revealed by the senses contains things which are both hard and soft. This is probably what Plato means in the seventh book of the *Republic*. Certainly he nowhere seems seriously to think that physical things in general lack definite properties or possess incompatible ones. The last argument in the *Phaedo* indeed takes it for granted that they cannot.[2]

But Plato might have said that physical things never are nor embody instances of the forms in a slightly different way. We have recently seen that forms were or tended to be the formal element in appropriate common natures. The form of circularity was perhaps the principle of unending self-consistency which is conformed to both by motion in a circle and also by

---

[1] EPD 2, pp. 284–305. [2] EPD, 2 p. 301.

rational thought[1]. But the best we meet with on earth is circular shapes; we never encounter unending self-consistency just on its own, expressed in no material. Therefore, what we find in physical things is not instances of forms but instances of forms-expressed-in-a-certain-matter. These we might call images of forms (as the *Timaeus* seems to call them) if we wanted to make the point that we can indeed re-activate our understanding of the rational principle expressed in such images, but can only do so if we try to peer through the expression to the principle expressed in it.

Plato's positive views upon the nature of the physical world are chiefly to be found in the *Theaetetus* and the *Timaeus* (both at least moderately late works); but what we find there is consistent with the doctrines expressed elsewhere if the more disparaging comments on the physical world in some dialogues are dealt with as we have just dealt with them. They seem to be along the following lines.

The physical world consists, as the Heracliteans said, of events. (By "the physical world" here I understand not the world of our sense-perceptions, but the world whose physical activity gives rise to our sense-perceptions by interacting with our sense-organs). It consists, therefore, of "flux", but it is essential to cap this by insisting also that things "flow" in determinate ways—so as to seem white to a normal percipient under normal conditions, for instance. Flux is therefore only a half-truth about the world, the persistence of pattern being equally important. The *Theaetetus* is non-committal on the nature of the events which constitute the flux, but it seems to assume that they consist of the travelling about, the collisions and so forth, of some kind of particles. The everyday empirical world of trees and sheep and men exists only in so far as it is perceived, being the product of the interaction between the particles external to us with those which constitute our sense-organs, or are emitted by them. A common-sense thing such as a stone is a collection of sense-perceptions, such collections arising when the activity of the particles in some region is sufficiently consistent to affect our senses more or less uniformly over a period of time. Since the world of sense-experience consists very

[1] *Laws* Bk. 10; EPD 2, p. 81.

largely of reasonably stable things, it follows presumably that the activity of the particles composing the physical world cannot be random, but must be governed by natural laws. But strictly speaking it could be said that there are no things or substances in the physical world, except perhaps the particles of which it is made. This is of course very much the account of the physical world which was given by Locke and other seventeenth-century writers and which was taken for granted by most scientists, at any rate until recently.

Plato was obviously not in a position to know anything about the nature of the ultimate constituents of matter or of the laws governing their behaviour. As a philosopher he contents himself with saying (in the *Theaetetus* and in the *Laws*) that the secondary qualities of things (their colour, taste and other sense-properties) must be dependent upon the primary qualities (size, shape, rest or motion, and other physical properties), or change of primary qualities, of something or other. But if he could know nothing about these matters, he could guess the more freely; and the *Timaeus* contains a number of such guesses. It offers us indeed a ramshackle and admittedly conjectural account, in outline terms, of pretty well everything.

Any theory which makes the world out of imperceptible particles runs into difficulties over what the particles are made of. The particles are ultimate—otherwise you go on *ad infinitum*. But now you are in a dilemma. The particles must occupy space—otherwise what does it mean to call them particles? But what do they occupy it with? To occupy space they must have size and shape, but how is whatever is inside their boundaries different from what is outside? You cannot say that the stuff of the particles is, for instance, grey, because the account that you have hitherto given of grey surfaces is, no doubt, that the particles composing them, or emitted by them, or something of the kind, are such as to interact by some physical means or other with our eyes so as to give rise to grey patches in our visual fields. Therefore, if you say that the particles themselves are grey, you will be forced to postulate further particles to compose the surfaces of the grey particles; and the same trouble will arise over these. The same trouble will also arise whatever sense-properties you attribute to your particles. What then can you attribute to them but primary qualities such as shape, size and motion, or resultants of these like some degree of elasticity, and so on? But in that case how do your particles differ from volumes—volumes of nothing-in-particular? And then why are they physical entities, and not merely geometrical? It is not indeed only a theory which uses particles which runs into this sort of trouble—waves are no better. Any theory which tries to construct an intuitable model of what lies behind the phenomena will want to measure the entities that it postulates, or give them conjectural measurements. Therefore, the entities in the model must have primary qualities; but equally they must not, if they are ultimate, have secondary qualities. Therefore, in the end any model builder, if asked what his measurements apply to, must answer with Locke: "Something, I know not what."

Plato seems to have taken this bull by the horns, whether or not he was explicitly aware of its menaces. For in the *Timaeus* the something, I know not what, of which the world is made is simply space. That at any rate is what it is called. It is, however, something a bit less tenuous than space, though it is emphasized that it must have no properties of its own in order that it may be capable of receiving all properties. But we are to understand that in its own nature and apart from the ordering work of mind it is capable of disorderly motion and indeed of forming itself into rude configurations reminiscent of the "knots in space" met with in popular expositions of relativity. The stuff of the physical world, then, is something that can be called space, is capable of disorderly motion and can form itself into rude shapes. This Plato takes to be eternal, coeval with the creative mind, or "Craftsman", and with the forms to which the Craftsman looks when he proceeds to impose order upon this chaos. When the Craftsman, of his benevolence, thinking order preferable to disorder, proceeds to the organization of chaos into cosmos, he begins by forming space into shapes guided to some extent by those it had formed of its own accord. Space as a whole he makes into a sphere, and in it he makes spherical bodies. That these may cohere he makes them out of four elements (earth, air, fire and water), the particles of each of which is a regular solid,[1] these in turn being made out of two fundamental shapes. The shapes which he chooses are two

---

[1] They are not solids of something, but just three-dimensional shapes.

triangles. These are the material out of which everything is made, the regular solids being as it were molecules and the triangles atoms. Since space as a whole is in restless motion the molecules are continually being thrown about, those with the most mobile shape (the pyramids) tending towards the periphery of the sphere into which the Craftsman has formed space, those with the least mobile shape (the cubes) tending towards the centre. Since the sphere is bounded, that which has tended outwards is forced back again as it approaches the boundary, and this keeps the whole process going indefinitely. Each of the four regular solids or molecules corresponds to one of the elements. Fire is made of pyramids, their sharp corners being destructive; earth, the most sluggish element, of cubes. Chemical change takes place through the effect which molecules of different shapes have on each other when they collide (they tend to slice each other into their component triangles, and these tend to re-combine into the same or different shapes). The physical properties of things—their elasticity for example—are due to the shapes of the molecules they are made of (i.e. to the proportion of the various elements in their constitution), their sense-properties to the interaction of their molecules upon those of the appropriate part of the body. The taste of a thing thus depends on how its particles fit the pores in the tongue, its colour on the size of the fiery particles emitted from its surface, and on their interaction with those emitted through the eyes. Everything, therefore, in one way or another is explained in terms of the dynamical properties of things in motion; these are the key to the extensive system of natural law which governs, it seems, pretty well everything that occurs.

Plato gives us then, as a conjecture, a deterministic account of nature in which his fundamental notions are space, shapes and motion. At the unsophisticated level the world consists of things—trees, rocks and so on; and these have their macroscopic behaviour-patterns. Trees grow, rocks stay still, milk goes sour and so on. These, however, are neither the basic entities nor the basic laws of nature. The sense-properties of physical things are products of the interaction between their components and those of our sense-organs. Since indeed we never observe in things anything but their sense-properties, common-sense things such as rocks can be regarded as collections of sense-data, provided we remember that our sense-data are caused by the activities of physical particles of some kind. It is upon the activities of these particles that the properties and behaviour-patterns of common-sense things depend. About the nature of these particles we can of course only conjecture. The conjecture offered in the *Timaeus* represents them as consisting of certain shapes. It seems likely that Plato did not expect us to take very seriously his suggestions as to what shapes these might be, but that he did expect us to take seriously the doctrine that the physical world consists ultimately of order imposed upon extension, and that, therefore, its elementary components must be geometrical entities, or in other words shapes. It is a valiant attempt to manage with three basic categories only: creative reason, the forms (the shapes of the particles being "images" of these), and space. Before dismissing as primitive the notion that the physical world can be thought of as a function of space and shape, ask a modern physicist what he supposes his waves and particles consist of.

Plato's views about the study of the physical world seems to be much what we might expect them to be. He sometimes speaks disparagingly of observation; in the seventh book of the *Republic* he tells us to ignore the "pretty things" in the sky when doing astronomy. Presumably he did not mean that science could dispense with *all* observation. Without any observation, the astronomer would not even know that there are any stars, nor could Timaeus have known what physical and chemical changes his atoms and molecules had to be used to explain. Plato's mistake, like that of many Greeks, was not to suppose that the facts can be collected with our eyes shut, but to suppose that they have all been collected. In that case what we need is not to get more observations, but to think about the ones we have got on the assumption that they make some kind of sense.

As to what kind of sense they make, it seems to depend on what department of nature we are considering. The *Timaeus* speaks, rather obscurely, about the natural world as the product of the collaboration of reason with necessity, or what had to be. The existence of space and its tendency to shake itself into rude shapes seem to be the contribution of necessity. This was what the Craftsman had to work upon in bringing into existence a tolerable state of affairs. A tolerable state of affairs seems to involve chiefly two things—the existence of living creatures and a certain ordered beauty in the whole creation and in as many of its components as possible. So we must suppose that the problem is posed for the Craftsman by the fact that space is what he has to work upon and by the fact that what he wants to make of it is an ordered environment for living creatures. Some of his dispositions directly realize these aims, others are instrumental to their realization. The stars move as they do because the dance that they perform is symbolic of the nature of intelligence, and is thus part of the beauty of the cosmos; human beings have livers not as an end in itself but because various moral purposes are thereby served. On the microscopic level the shapes of the molecules are regular because regularity is better than irregularity, but doubtless many of the details of their sizes and disposition in space are simply chosen because their choice facilitates some arrangement having moral or aesthetic value.

If, therefore, we are inquiring into some question such as why milk turns sour or why prunes are laxative, the best we can do is to tell some likely story (knowing that it is no more than a guess) which makes sense in terms of the assumption that creative intelligence will have made the microscopic arrangements both orderly and also as economical and efficient as possible, and also in terms of the general ends of creation. We shall have to bear in mind, in this, that much of what happens is doubtless allowed to happen as a necessary by-product in the realization of something else. Smells for example, Timaeus seems to suggest, are really only there because, when a molecule is broken up into its component triangles, these do not always properly re-combine into fresh regular solids, and these *disiecta membra* affect our nasal membranes in different ways. Still, wherever a teleological virtue could be made of a necessity, it will have been. Thus hair is a kind of excrement made of surplus body fluids; but the necessity of excreting these has been turned to good use by guiding the waste chiefly to the head, where it serves to protect the brain. The student, therefore, of terrestrial phenomena, and particularly the biologist, should always have his eye open for some function which whatever he is studying may perform; and this, if he finds it, is what he must cite as the cause of the phenomenon. But he must also bear in mind that the effects which reason brings about are brought about through the regular behaviour of the elementary particles of which things are made, and that this will inevitably produce on the macroscopic level some effects which are not desirable, but neutral or even bad.

Fire, however, is a docile kind of stuff; you can make what you want of it. Therefore, in the region of the universe where fire and air are what one chiefly encounters one ought to expect few or no phenomena which reason has not produced for their own sake. The astronomer in other words is studying objects whose behaviour can be expected to express directly the nature of reason. Something similar, as it happens, is true of the musician, for sound, like fiery bodies, is something which can be made to express rational order; and it may be, Plato more than once suggests, that there are other sets of terrestrial phenomena to which the same applies. With regard to astronomy Plato's views seem to have undergone some change; or perhaps he came to believe what he had only hoped. In the *Republic* Socrates tells us that the stars, being physical, cannot be expected to keep time perfectly. However, he seems to suggest, if we do not fuss too much about where precisely the stars are at any given moment, and if we are skilled enough mathematicians, we can trace out the figure that the stars ought to dance even though in fact they dance it clumsily. In the *Timaeus* and *Laws*, however, and in the *Epinomis* (an appendix to the *Laws* whose authenticity some dispute), the pessimism has vanished; indeed the punctuality of the stars is an argument for the divine government of the universe. This no doubt reflects the actual progress of astronomy. Eudoxus, a colleague of Plato in the Academy, managed to produce an account of planetary motions (some say in response to a challenge by Plato), which made it seem reasonable to hope that it could be shown that the planets do in fact travel in regular orbits, and not wander aimlessly as they appear to do. In that case faith could hold to the proposition that the movement of the heavens is in accordance with an enormously complicated pattern which symbolizes the nature of reason, and that this symbolism could be read by one of sufficient mathematical equipment. The *Timaeus* indeed flatly

declares that this is the case. It makes the disposition of the stars
conform to musical intervals in a way too elaborate to describe.
(Presumably the reason for this is that ordered harmony is
expressed both in music and in the heavens, and therefore the
same structure will hold in both; since we can study this structure in musical harmony, we learn of it there and extrapolate it
to astronomy). It also postulates two rotations in the heavens;
one of the whole heavens in one direction, the other a set of
seven rotations in the contrary sense, one for each of the objects
which travel round the earth, viz. the sun, moon and five
planets.[1] These rotations are called that of sameness and that of
difference. The suggestion is, I think, that the function of this
feature of the astronomical dance is to symbolize the two
essential moments of intelligence: the rotation of sameness
our ability to identify, that of difference our ability to
differentiate.

This illustrates, indeed, the difference between the ancient
and the modern world; but it also illustrates how Plato thought
the study of astronomy ought to be carried on. It is unjust to say
that he thought astronomy ought to be done *a priori*, if that
means that it ought to be done by deduction from self-evident
premises. He is obviously trying in the *Timaeus* to offer an
account which is faithful to the observed facts; but the point is
that it is to be an account of them that makes sense—and you
determine what counts as sense by asking what ends the force
responsible for the ordered cosmos could have sought to realize.
Copernicus also wanted an account of the heavens that made
sense, and so do Hoyle and Ryle when they argue for continuous creation or the "big bang". Only, their conceptions of
what makes sense differ—from each other and from Plato's. It
is at this point that cosmology and metaphysics are most closely
connected.

We can ask how Plato thought one was to determine what is
to count as sense. On this he seems, at one time at any rate, to
have had a definite answer. In the *Republic* the crown of philosophic achievement is the vision of the good; this means I think
that the crown of philosophic achievement is to divine what

---

[1] Plato's universe is spherical and geocentric. He seems to have imputed movement of some kind to the earth, but if it does not stay precisely in the centre, it is at
any rate revolved around.

F   71

goodness, or congruence to reason, consists in.[1] The *Republic* is the only place where Plato puts forward the odd, though characteristic, view that the last thing the mind can look at is the source of the light by which it sees; and he may not have persisted in it. But so long as he did, he would doubtless have said that nobody strictly speaking could know what dispositions are "for the best" who has not "seen the good"—meaning by this that nobody could have full confidence in his judgment of what makes sense until he had seen how everything coheres. Meanwhile, though, there are other questions which the Platonic scientist can ask. The creative intelligence does not determine the behaviour of the things it creates without reference to their nature. The behaviour of things, therefore, in so far as it conforms to their maker's purposes, will be consistent with what they are. It seems to me that the *Phaedo* suggests that, if you want to determine cosmological astronomical questions, you must do so on the presupposition that reason will have disposed things for the best; and that it hints that to make use of this presupposition you must ask what the entity that you are studying is. If for example you think that a star is just a lump of matter, you will have no clue to its probable motions, and any account of astronomical observations will be as good as any other. If, however, you see that a star is an intelligent being with a body of fire (a conclusion you can come to by reflecting on the proposition that the creative intelligence will have peopled the cosmos, so far as possible, with rational beings, so that these may share the work of keeping orderly the physical realm), then you will be predisposed to attribute to the stars that motion which expresses the principle of endless self-consistency—i.e. motion in a circle. Doubtless similar considerations will apply to some extent when one is considering the behaviour of other products of reason such as human beings. Since, however, these are at once more complicated and more readily observable than stars, the question "What is a man?" is likely to be less fruitful in anthropology than the question "What is a star?" ought to be in astronomy.

It can be seen now that certain modifications are needed in things we said earlier. I suggested that strictly speaking it might be said that the physical world contains no things or

[1] EPD 2, pp. 171 sqq.

substances except perhaps the particles whose interaction with those of our sense-organs gives rise to sense-data, and thus to the familiar world which consists of the patterns into which these fall. And certainly in his earlier writings Plato seems anxious to deny to physical things the status of *onta* or ultimate realities; the physical world is a sphere of *genesis*, becoming or process, and its contents are *gignomena*, things that become. This is entirely consistent with the view that the tree in the quad is really a logical construction out of the sense-events which occur when the particles of people's eyes (and hands and so on) are disturbed by the activity of the particles occupying the region of space where the tree is said to be. There is a passage in the *Timaeus*[1] which seems to suggest that strictly speaking one ought never to talk of things (for nouns and noun-surrogates like "thing" connote a misleading degree of stability), but always only of regions of space characterized by certain qualities, as if this rock is the greyness, roughness, warmth and so on which characterize, at the moment, this place. (Timaeus, however, is about to talk about his elementary particles and I daresay he is not primarily concerned with macroscopic things; though as he speaks of steam condensing into water and solidifying into ice, he certainly has them in mind).

But this sort of view of the world is, notoriously, incomplete, if only because it has to mention *people*; and, though human bodies *can* be treated as systems of particles like any other, sense cannot be made of human beings as observers unless we emphasize also the unity which results from the system; and if we do this for human beings, why not for horses and hollyhocks? In other words whatever the stuff of the world may be, the world itself consists of ordered centres of activity far above the level of atoms and molecules; and these centres of activity, these moles and weasels, sycamores and men, are not just phenomenally real unities like rainbows or the black mouths of tunnels; they are ultimate unities. There may be some things in the phenomenal world—lumps of mud for example—which are just families of sense-data created by the activity of more or less disorganized particles; but very many of its contents are real unitary systems, the behaviour of their component particles being so determined that it preserves the system in existence.

[1] *Timaeus* 49–50. EPD i, pp. 44–5.

More cosmologically put, creative reason did not just order the stuff of physical extension into its regular shapes and leave these to make what impact they might in the sense-fields of disembodied observers; it brought into being, or continuously brings into being, a world of living things and of the inanimate objects which constitute their environment. Macroscopic physical things may be, in one way, resultants of the interaction of unobservable particles, but they are not in the least fictions, like corporate personality, phenomena, like rainbows, nor illusions, like Macbeth's dagger. Plato may perhaps have been reluctant for some time to concede enough weight to considerations such as these, but justice is done to them in the cosmological parts of his later writings. This is marked indeed in the *Philebus* by a significant shift in his use of the terms *genesis* ("becoming") and *ousia* ("being"). In the *Republic* for example these words can be used as nicknames for the physical world and for the entities with which abstract intelligence deals. (This does not carry the implication that the physical world is "unreal", though it does carry the implication that all ultimate entities belong to the latter class. But it is perfectly consistent with the view that physical things are systems of unobservable particles ordered in accordance with rational principles). But in the *Philebus* the word *ousia* is used for anything which intelligence, cosmic or human, brings into being, *genesis* being used for the process by which it is brought into being. Perhaps what had happened is that the belief that the world is, by and large, a product of reason, a belief which was stifled to some extent by Heraclitean doctrines of flux and Orphic-Pythagorean disdain for the body, had managed to fight its way up to the light and receive an expression in Plato's language commensurate with the influence it had always exercised on his thought.

5

Spiritual Things

THAT the spiritual is prior to the physical is the conviction that always animated Plato's philosophy. But this is not to say that he maintained one monolithic doctrine on the subject from the beginning. We are to remember always that Plato conceived of philosophy as an almost unending struggle to give satisfactory expression to what, in one sense, we know perfectly well all along.

There was no body of doctrinal orthodoxy in religion among the Greeks, except in so far as the Homeric poems provided it; but in fact they provided little more for the educated than the accepted vocabulary in which one talked about the divine. You spoke of Zeus if you meant the supreme government of the universe, of Aphrodite if you meant the supernatural forces which are expressed in love. In so far as one could be orthodox, the Platonic Socrates seems to have been an orthodox Athenian in matters of religion. More than some of his contemporaries, he objected to the anthropomorphism of the Homeric poems, and the unprincipled behaviour of Homer's gods, as corrupt expressions of the divine; and he shows perhaps more sympathy than was popular with the Orphic and Pythagorean dichotomy between the soul and the body, with their belief that the discarnate existence of the soul is altogether better than incarnation in the body, and with their belief that such incarnations will continue until by purity of living one earns escape from the cycle of rebirth. But he talks indifferently of God, the gods, the god, the divine; and he calls the gods from time to time by their appropriate names. He is in fact a polytheist with

75

no very explicit theology except that which he adopts from time to time from the Orphics and Pythagoreans; and this he is always rather tentative about.

The religious atmosphere, therefore, of Plato's earlier writings is fairly orthodox. There are gods, they have some concern with, and influence upon human affairs. Plato is, as most of his educated contemporaries probably were, sceptical of the Homeric mythology, and of the cult-practices which were supposed to achieve tangible benefits—charms, purifications, soothsayings and so on. But he does not seem to question the existence of a distinct race of superhuman beings with fairly extensive powers of intervention in the universe. Nor are there in the earlier writings any unequivocal declarations of the doctrine that the physical universe owes its existence to the divine, though there are doubtless hints of it in the *Republic*. The most distinctive feature of that part of Plato's religious beliefs which he reveals in the earlier dialogues is the heavy moral emphasis, the emphasis both on the moral purity of the divine beings, and on the demands which they make upon man. There is also a suggestion that men can become more like the gods, and that the gods are somehow on the side of those who try to do so. Moral purity and the pursuit of wisdom are the chief means to this end, but prayer, and from the other side some kind of inspiration, are not excluded.

Man is, as in the Orphic-Pythagorean tradition, a soul housed in a body. Life, says the *Phaedo*, is the marriage of soul and body, death their divorce; and a blessed release. The soul is immortal, has pre-existed our birth and will survive our death—except that some provision seems to be made for the annihilation of incurably wicked souls. The soul's immortality is inferable, in the *Phaedo*, chiefly from two things, primarily from the fact that a soul is that which can animate a body, less conclusively from the fact that the soul is akin to the forms, the objects of eternal reason. At death the soul can expect to enjoy a period of discarnate existence, during which it will be judged and perhaps punished to purge it of the stains of its earthly wrong-doings. Eventually, however, the souls of all but those who have loved wisdom single-mindedly will be incarnated once more, not necessarily in human bodies but in whatever

76

bodily form their conduct during their last incarnation has rendered appropriate.⌉(In the *Republic* the souls actually choose the lives they are to live, the point being that the choice a man makes reveals his character).

Most of this doctrine is to be found in the "myths" or grand eschatological parables with which Plato tries to drive home his teaching in the *Gorgias, Phaedo* and *Republic*; but enough of it is to be found in the non-mythical part of the *Phaedo* to make it fair to say that Plato at least thought it decent to impute these beliefs to Socrates. How far he shared them himself it is difficult to say; indeed he frequently makes Socrates say, not that these things are ascertainably true, but that they are "likely stories" told to him by "priests . . . who have tried to understand their priesthood" and so on. One suspects—I find it hard to see with what justification—that Plato's ideas were more sophisticated and more evasive than those he imputes to Socrates, despite his obvious admiration for and sympathy with the simplicity and directness of the latter's piety.

But at any rate, even if Plato did not think that the virtuous bourgeois is at all likely to be reincarnated, as Socrates suggests in the *Phaedo*, in the body of an ant, he obviously did believe that the soul is something distinct from the body and that it is immortal, and therefore an eternal thing which did not come into existence at the moment of birth. What exactly Plato took the soul to be is not so clear. In the *Phaedo* it is officially that which animates a body; but it is tacitly assumed both that this is something rational, and that it is something personal, i.e. something capable of desires, emotions, purposes. It is not precisely identical with the whole of a man's personal life, for the *Phaedo* attributes carnal desires, and also such emotion as anger and fear, to the body. On the other hand the soul is not to be identified with that part of personal life which is thought to be capable of eternal life. This does indeed exclude the bodily passions, but it excludes too much. Socrates makes it clear in the *Phaedo* (and what he says is endorsed by Timaeus and by the Athenian Stranger in the *Laws*) that *eventually* the system of reincarnation is to purify the soul of everything except its "philosophic part"—that by virtue of which a man can take delight in truth, beauty and wisdom. But in the meantime the soul seems to be not just the philosophic part, but rather that part of

Spiritual Things

his personal life with which a man identifies himself. In so far as he resists his less rational propensities they are "the body"; if he inclines towards anger or towards greed these passions, though of bodily origin, become a "carnal accretion" upon his soul; and when he dies he will miserably persist as one who retains impulses which he is no longer able to gratify. Identification in this way, with the interests of the body is that from which a soul must be purified; the philosopher seeks such purification in life by eschewing the senses, the gods impose it upon all except hopeless cases after death by purgatorial treatment in the discarnate condition, and by suitable reincarnation subsequently. That which survives death, then, is the personality which a man has built for himself in life; that which is strictly eternal is the philosophic part of this.

The doctrine of the philosophic part and the carnal accretion developed in the *Republic* and *Timaeus* into the well-known doctrine of the tripartite soul, a version of which is depicted in the myth of the *Phaedrus* in the figure of the charioteer driving two horses, one tame and noble, the other lustful and unruly. The doctrine is that every soul consists of three parts, the rational or calculative, the spirited, and the appetitive. The rational is that with which a man pursues truth and consults his real best interests, the spirited that element of self-respect by which he is enabled to behave aggressively both towards outward enemies and towards his own baser impulses, the appetitive is his susceptibility to organic satisfactions; and the behaviour associated with each of these three principles is named after it. Thus acting prudently or discussing philosophy is the work of the rational part, fighting a duel belongs to the spirited part; and earning money belongs to the appetitive part, sometimes also called the acquisitive.

The essence of the doctrine is probably as follows. A soul is in its own true nature a lover of truth, order and harmony. This is for Plato the kernel of personal existence. The endeavour of every soul is to reproduce these qualities wherever it can; for souls are all of one kind, whether divine, human or sub-human, though there are better and worse among them, and this determines what kind of body each animates. A soul then is essentially a lover and reproducer of reason, order and harmony. This being the case the method employed by the creative mind to

78

bring order into the physical universe is to create living creatures, unions of soul and body. The hardest task is borne by those souls whose lot it is to be united with bodies made of grosser material, and to keep order in the earthy parts of the world. When a soul is thrust into a human body two things happen to it. First it receives a considerable shock; its "revolutions" (its endlessly self-consistent intellectual activity) are dislocated, disturbed by the flux of sense-perceptions which must pour in upon it if it is to find its bearings in the station of life to which it has been called. Secondly, in order that it may behave appropriately in that station, it must be given new impulses which have nothing to do with its native impulse towards truth and order. In order that it may want to preserve in being the body which it animates, and reproduce a supply of such bodies for other souls to animate, it must become susceptible to organic desires, these being things of physical status but of carnal origin in the sense that their *raison d'être* is related only to the purposes of incarnation. Again in order that it may fight when appropriate against other animals which are behaving unjustly, and also at all times against its own temptations to such behaviour, it must receive a further set of psychic susceptibilities having little to do with the essential interests of reason, those comprehended under the notions of pride, spirit and self-respect. A human personality thus becomes something more complicated, and much more potentially tumultuous, than a soul is in its true essence. The task for man is to "re-establish the revolutions" of his soul, to recapture the love of wisdom and harmony alone which is his proper activity, disregarding all other impulses except in so far as they indicate to him what his duty, as one responsible for the good order of a corner of the universe, happens at any moment to be. The *Timaeus* (in which, along with the *Phaedrus* and tenth book of the *Laws*, the thoughts in this paragraph are to be found) makes a sharp division between the love of wisdom on the one hand and all other human propensities on the other, by calling the first the immortal part of the soul, the rest the mortal. It locates the immortal part in the head, dividing the mortal part between spirit in the chest and appetite in the belly. (It does not of course intend to identify the part of the soul with the region of the body in which it locates it, but to suggest that the activity of the organs in that region is the vehicle of the activity of that part). It drives the distinction home by attributing the creation of the immortal part of the soul to the creator of the universe, who uses in its creation the same materials as he used for the souls of the universe and of the mortal gods,[1] while the mortal part is the work of the mortal god (in other words the planet) on which the soul arises. Human souls, then, consist partially of something eternal and of divine origin, this being the rational propensities and activities which use the brain as their organ; but they consist also of certain other propensities and activities which are of humbler origin in that their existence is necessitated by the existence of the body which the soul is in charge of, and in that they are very closely connected with the activities of the bodily organs. In so far as these propensities are accepted and endorsed by the rational part, which is a man's true self, they persist (or the disorder which they create persists) as part of his soul even after death has destroyed their utility; but their ultimate fate is to be eliminated.

We have been drawing upon the later dialogues in order to illuminate the treatment of the soul to be found in the earlier ones. The justification for doing this is that it seems that Plato's religious views are in general not very fully expressed in his earlier writings. He seems to have used a certain economy of truth. Perhaps it would have been impolitic to say too much; Socrates after all had been prosecuted for impiety. Doubtless Plato's views developed; but there is some indication even in the earlier writings that the fairly simple orthodox belief in the existence of a race of superior beings of a more or less anthropomorphic kind does not do justice to Plato's theology. There is for example the insistence on the immutability of the divine in the *Republic*, and the odd figure in the tenth book of the same dialogue where God is spoken of as the maker of the form of a bed. This is, doubtless, figurative, but it suggests more of a doctrine of divine creation than Socrates is usually made to profess.

The religious atmosphere of the later dialogues is in some

[1] For more about these, see below. The materials used for the creation of human souls are the same, but they are "what he had left over", i.e. they are of poorer quality.

ways rather puzzling. We find considerable emphasis on the primacy of the spiritual. We find passages which seem to confess an almost Hebraic faith in God as the creator of all things. But it would probably be a bad mistake to interpret all this in Hebraic or Christian terms.

If the earlier dialogues give the impression that their author subscribed to a fairly orthodox pagan polytheism, the later dialogues sometimes seem to have almost pantheist elements. Whereas in the Judaeo-Christian tradition the cleavage always comes between God and the world, in Plato the cleavage is between the spiritual and the physical—souls on the one hand, body on the other. The difference between human and divine souls is one of quality only, not one of kind; divine souls are thoroughbreds. It is not, however, at all clear how much Plato intends to imply when he imputes to something a soul. The reason for hesitation on this point is the levity with which Plato seems to postulate the existence of souls. Roughly speaking whatever persists in activity which is not imposed upon it by something else is said to have a soul; and this naturally makes one wonder whether by "soul" Plato intends more than "self-activating activity". (Indeed the definition of the soul in the *Phaedrus* and the *Laws* is in terms of approximately that phrase).

In the mythical representation of Plato's cosmology in the *Timaeus* the range of spiritual beings is as follows. (1) There is first the Craftsman, eternal, uncreated, creative reason, coeval with the forms and with brute matter or "space". The Craftsman has no body; all bodies are his handiwork. (2) Comprehending all other bodies is the universe itself; it can be called a body because it is a physical system. Accordingly the first spiritual being the Craftsman creates is a soul to animate the body of the universe. The things that Timaeus says about the creation of this *anima mundi* are extremely obscure, but he seems to try to endow it with what it needs to understand, so to speak, how to bring about unceasingly that astronomical disposition of its bodily parts whereby their motions symbolize the nature of reason. We are naturally, therefore, tempted to think that the soul of the universe is quite simply the fact that the heavenly bodies do dispose themselves in an orderly and harmonious manner. (The Craftsman reappears in the *Statesman* and also, as it seems, in the *Philebus* and in *Laws* Book Ten. The soul of the

universe, however, is not mentioned elsewhere). (3) Next after
the soul of the universe we have the souls of the mortal gods;[1]
these are, primarily at any rate, the souls which animate the
bodies of whose motions the universe consists—in other words
the heavenly bodies. Here again we are naturally tempted to
identify these souls simply with the propensity of their bodies to
conform to their orbits. However, in *Laws* 12 and in the
Epinomis[2] it is argued that without intelligence the stars could not
keep time so marvellously, and in *Laws* 10 the question is raised
whether the soul of the sun propels its body from within or from
without, or in some other incomprehensible way. These
passages seem to suggest that the soul of a heavenly body is
something other than the fact that that body is always where it
should be, though it does not require too much ingenuity to
construe them otherwise. (Could not "without intelligence the
stars could not keep time" be construed as "time-keeping is by
definition intelligent; intelligence just *is* getting things right"?).
(4) Next after the souls of the mortal gods we have the souls of
lesser mortal creatures; here, as in the *Phaedrus* and the *Epinomis*,
the point is made that these are of the same "material" as the
souls of the gods, though inferior in quality. They range from
the souls of men (i.e. masculine humans; women are animated
by souls which did not do very well in their previous incarnation), through the souls of animals, to the souls of plants
which are "vegetative only"—whatever that may mean.

Among all these spiritual beings one class stands out; the
souls of human beings. For we have the best of reasons for
saying that talking about human personality is not just an
oblique way of talking about the behaviour of human bodies.
Are we to infer that Plato seriously thought that stars and dor-
mice were animated by something closely akin to human personality? Or did he simply regard the capacity for self-activa-
tion as the essential feature of human personality so that one
could without any ambiguity impute a soul to whatever activates
itself? Were consciousness, emotion, desire merely accidents,
perhaps impediments, to human personality, or were these to
be found in the stars? Did Plato believe in the existence of

[1] "Mortal" here means "created and therefore theoretically destructible; but
not in fact likely to be destroyed."
[2] See above, p. 70.

various superhuman personalities, or did he, with Bishop Robinson, merely wish to give figurative expression to the sentiment that reality is ultimately personal, or ultimately rational? Certainly Plato talks (in *Laws* 10) of "spiritual activities such as beliefs, desires and fears" being primary in the cosmos; but of course with a little behaviouristic analysis of such notions (so that desire, for example, becomes propensity to do) we can easily treat such language as figurative. The *Epinomis* expresses a positive lack of interest in the Olympians. (The *Timaeus* had also been sarcastic about "the gods who appear in people's family trees". As a descendant of Poseidon Plato was doubtless entitled to use such sarcasm). But it expresses sympathy with the doctrine that "all things are full of gods." Whatever is capable of living, it tells us, has been given a soul and made to live. There are therefore living creatures at every level of the universe, from the stars in the fiery region downwards,[1] including a new race of demi-gods who inhabit the region of *aithêr* or "pure air", which the Stranger postulates, and who, with their colleagues of the lower air, act as intermediaries between all living organisms. They are capable of pleasure and pain (the high gods, it is implied in this passage, are not susceptible to these), they know our thoughts, we encounter them in dreams and visions, and it is these encounters that have given rise to the traditional cults.

What are we to make of all this? The passage from the *Epinomis* is difficult to de-mythologize, for it seems itself to be engaged in de-mythologizing the official cults. The *Epinomis* may possibly not be authentic, though it seems at the very least to have been written by somebody who supposed himself to understand Plato's mind. But there are other passages in *Laws* 10 and elsewhere which are cumulatively hard to soothe away. In the *Phaedrus*, commenting on a traditional legend, Socrates says that demythologizing is often easy, but he finds it ungracious. Does he mean merely that it destroys the beauty of the stories, or does he also think that something of truth is thereby also lost?

We want to press such questions as whether Plato conceived of the stars as some kind of personal beings, whether his creative God was an individual personal substance transcending the

---

[1] Metaphorically downwards; the universe is spherical.

universe or rather merely the fact that rational order is immanent in it. We would like to know whether the warfare which the gods wage in *Laws* 10 on behalf of virtue is an actual influence exerted by actual divine beings, or whether it is to be understood simply as the fact that the ultimate structure of the universe favours virtue and penalizes vice. We would like to ask whether Plato really believes, as he sometimes seems to, in two orders, the supernatural and the natural, with the former intervening in the course of the latter. Perhaps, however, we are wrong to press such questions. The final argument for immortality in the *Phaedo* works by treating a fact (being alive) as if it were at the same time an individual (a soul). We are inclined to dismiss this at once as a category-mistake. The category-distinction which we rely on to do this—that between concrete individuals and abstract entities such as facts—is one that we owe ultimately to Plato, to his distinction between forms and their instances. Perhaps, however, even he found it difficult to carry this distinction right up to the highest levels of theology. There are after all notorious difficulties in treating God as a transcendent individual. How can one have an individual where one cannot individuate, and how can one individuate when there is no body that one can point to as that to which one is referring? How, therefore, can one speak of something beyond the physical universe? On the other hand there are for a theist equal difficulties in treating God as anything but a transcendent individual. If God is a mere aspect of the universe (its being ultimately rational or something of the kind), how can this be responsible for anything? Surely it is at least as much of a category-mistake to speak of one aspect of something as generating all the other facts about it as it is to speak of an individual which is not a physical thing. Aristotle seems to have had it both ways. Perhaps the right answer to our questions about Plato is that he too is having it both ways, only more vaguely, less explicitly, more evasively if you wish, than Aristotle.

At any rate we can sum up the religious position of the later dialogues in something like the following way. We will proceed by preserving an essential vagueness in the notion of a soul. A soul is a source of rational order—a centre by which it is apprehended and from which it is propagated; whether such a centre is simply the orderliness of the physical system whose orderly behaviour leads us to speak of its soul, or something which transcends it, is the question we will leave unanswered. We begin then with the Craftsman, with the creative reason responsible for the order of the universe. Whether this being is to be spoken of as a soul is difficult to say. Generally speaking a soul corresponds to a body, which would suggest the answer No. A passage in the *Philebus*, however, saying that you cannot have intelligence without soul, suggests the answer Yes.[1] However this may be, all other souls depend upon this being; in the mythical account in the *Timaeus* they are all created by the Craftsman, either directly or through his creatures as intermediaries, which must mean that they are ontologically dependent upon the existence of creative reason. All souls, however, are in practice immortal—destructible by divine power only, and not likely to be destroyed. Coeval with the Craftsman there are the forms or rational principles which he apprehends, and there is also "space". The method by which the Craftsman proceeds in imposing order on the physical realm is to create within it souls to animate and preserve in orderly behaviour the physical bodies which can be formed in it. Being immortal, only a finite supply of these is needed, for they can be used again when their bodies wear out. Since, apparently, the physical realm cannot be made into a system of bodies of uniformly excellent docility (that matter has a brute recalcitrance which obstinately resists the demands of reason seems to be a persistent strand in Plato's thought),[2] it is necessary that bodies of varying degrees of complexity should be created, from the stars which consist of fire to the earth which consists of all the elements. Therefore there must be souls of varying degrees of complexity from the unimpeded and therefore "divine" souls of the stars downwards to those of brutes in which the presence of reason is residual and the pressure of the "mortal parts" paramount. Among those souls whose proper activity is impeded by the recalcitrance of their bodies there is the possibility of moral progress and degeneration, and therefore the possibility that some given soul may have become unfitted, when the body which it has animated ceases to be a viable living system, to animate another body of

[1] *Philebus* 29–30.
[2] It is expressed especially clearly in the myth in the *Statesman*.

the same kind, and will therefore be employed upon the animation of some other, higher or lower as the case may be.

It is difficult to decide how all of this is to be accommodated to the intimations which we find in the earlier dialogues of belief in providence, in rewards and punishments both temporal and eschatological, in the value of prayer and the possibility of divine inspiration. All of these are preserved in the tenth book of the *Laws*; but whereas in the earlier dialogues Socrates sometimes speaks as if the gods are to be thought of as intervening in the natural order, the *Laws* seems to try to reduce these "interventions" to standing features of the natural order. One can say that the gods fight against vice, but this seems to mean that vice attracts its own penalties. Again it is difficult to decide how the hope of personal immortality which Socrates tentatively expresses in the *Apology* and vindicates in the *Phaedo* is to be reconciled with the view (present in the *Phaedo*) that what is of eternal significance in the soul is not personality but rationality. Plato never entirely abandons belief in personal values. Love, joy, peace seem to be characteristic of the existence of those blameless philosophic souls who escape from the circle of rebirth to the islands of the blessed. On the other hand what they love and delight in seems to be largely intelligible truths.

The truth probably is that Plato never really reconciled his belief in the dignity of human existence with his belief that nothing physical is of any ultimate worth. A human personality cannot be winkled out of its body as easily as Plato supposed; a human being is a more corporeal thing than his dichotomy of soul and body allows for. The belief that God did not create the physical realm, but merely reduced it to order, makes it easy for Plato to deal with the problem of evil; for whatever is unsatisfactory can be attributed to the poverty of the material on which reason was obliged to work. But it also makes it all too easy for Plato to find incarnate existence ultimately valueless. Souls are thrust into bodies, in the end, so that they may help in the work of maintaining order in the cosmos. Apart from that duty, like the rulers in Socrates' Republic, they would sooner spend their time contemplating truths. This means that human life as we know it is in itself valueless, and gives us a very different religious attitude from any that is based on the saying in *Genesis*: "Let us make man in our image."

It might perhaps be pertinently added that Plato's failure to make theoretical sense of man's terrestrial existence fits very well with the disdainful attitude to useful employment which seems to have been common to Greek intellectuals; though Socrates it should be observed is, even in Plato's pages, something of an exception to this. It is also of course poetically congenial with Heraclitean notions of flux.

6

Perception and Knowledge

so far we have been considering Plato's account of objective reality. We have seen that he represents the physical universe as a product of two factors—of the divine (intelligences and the intelligible principles which they apprehend), operating upon and immanent in that which is in its own nature indeterminate extension, or "space". Without space there would be no physical things, though there would still exist the rational principles to which their design conforms; without the efficacy of intelligence the physical realm would consist of "an indeterminate sea of dissimilarity" (*Statesman*), a restless coming and going of entities too formless to be classified; too momentary, even, to count as entities.

We are now to turn our attention to Plato's account of our knowledge of objective reality. We shall be pre-disposed to expect that his account will represent our grasp of intelligible principles as something which is, potentially, much more intimate than our grasp of their embodiment in physical material can ever hope to be. This expectation will not be disappointed. But we should not suppose that Plato had from the beginning and retained to the end a fully worked-out theory of knowledge expressible in such simple formulas as *that knowledge is of the forms*, and *that there can be no knowledge of physical things*. We know already that there is a sense in which everything we can ever come to understand is something which we have at all times already learnt, and we can infer from this that nothing which we owe to empirical observation will ever give us ultimate insight. That which we owe to empirical observation is that which we have to try to understand; it cannot contribute to the light through which our understanding is done. The physical world is the problem; the mind must provide the answers out of its own resources. But although we are entitled to expect that Plato's discussions of knowledge will be conducted within this framework, we have no right to expect that they will simply plug the framework, and we shall misunderstand them if we do expect this. The truth is that in most of his discussions Plato is considering, and groping his way towards solving, problems which arise within this framework.

Let us begin with the *Theaetetus* and its account of our knowledge of the external world. Badgered by Socrates to produce a definition of knowledge, Theaetetus suggests that knowledge is perception; what we know, we perceive, and what we perceive, we know. What makes this definition plausible (for we do not see or smell that $2+2=4$) is the elasticity, in Greek as in English, of the verbs for *to perceive*. Protagoras, persuaded of the Parmenidean argument that there can be no false propositions, had tried to defend the view that every belief is true. In doing this it seems that he had traded upon the elasticity of verbs of the *perceive*-family. His argument essentially was (as Plato represents it) that since no man ever reports on anything but his own private world, and since a man's private world is constituted by what appears to him, therefore every opinion must be true since every opinion must be part of what appears to the man whose opinion it is, and this is the only thing against which an opinion can be measured. Therefore, there can be good opinions and bad opinions (those which lead respectively to desirable and undesirable results), but there can be no false opinions. Plato's diagnosis of the fallacy in this argument seems to be that Protagoras starts from the plausible proposition that the world of a man's sense-perceptions is private, and proceeds from this to the unplausible assumption that the world which each man inhabits is private. That which "appears" in the sense-perception usage of this word is indeed private in the sense that you do not see identically the same view that I see (but I see my view and you yours), and indeed that the view that you see may not be very like the view that I see, even if we are viewing from the same point. But the world consists not just of views, smells, sounds and so on, but of the patterns into which these fall. We cannot, from the fact that sense-data (or that which "appears" perceptually) are private, infer that that which "appears" in the judgment-usage of the word is also private. If the wine "appears" (i.e. tastes) sour to me, then the wine is sour-to-me. But if the wine "appears" likely to please you, it does not follow that the wine will please you. The rock, therefore, on which Plato breaks Protagoras' doctrine that "whatever seems to a man, is to that man" is that judgments about the future are not infallible. The reason why they are not infallible is, no doubt, that judgment about the future (and the same is true about all judgments which are more than reports of immediate perception) are interpretations of the significance of the sense-perceptions which a man receives, and thus transcend the private world of sense-experience. If they did not purport to comment upon the objective world they could not claim the status of truths or items of knowledge; if they do purport to comment upon it then they cannot claim infallibility on the ground that they relate merely to a man's private world. Socrates' argument therefore has in effect the form of a dilemma:— If by "perception" you mean sense-perception, or reports upon it, then these cannot claim the status of knowledge, for such reports make no comment upon the objective world; but if by "perception" you mean judgments which comment upon the objective world, then these cannot claim the incorrigibility which is owned by reports of immediate perception. This rebuttal of Protagoras' argument disentangles most admirably the sensory and intellectual elements in our knowledge of the external world. It makes the point that hearing, for example, what you say is not just an achievement of one of my senses. My hearing gives me sounds; but that gives me no information until, at the very least, my mind records that I am hearing sounds; and I do not get much information which is any use to me (Theaetetus makes this point in terms of the example of hearing people talking in a foreign language), until my mind interprets the significance of the sounds by correctly detecting their similarity to other sounds heard on other occasions.

In order to arrive at this position Socrates suggests that Theaetetus' Protagorean equation of knowledge with perception involves a certain theory of sense-perception which in turn involves a Heraclitean account of the physical world. What Socrates appears to do is to accept the account of sense-perception, while resisting Protagoras' extrapolations from it to the sphere of judgment in general, and to accept the part of the Heraclitean account of the physical world which the account of sense-perception properly involves, while rejecting the further Heraclitean doctrines which tended to support the parts of Protagoras' doctrine which are unacceptable. Plato is thus disentangling what is true and what is false in the Heraclitean tradition, and, in doing so, stating for the first time an account of the external world and of our knowledge of it which has been perhaps the most popular account of these matters since the rise of the scientific movement in the seventeenth century.[1]

Roughly, the Heraclitean tradition had insisted that *everything* is impermanent; there is *no* stability of any kind. Not only must the things of common sense be analysed away into series of events; it must also be said that strictly speaking there is no stability in the succession of events. Not only does the existence of a physical thing consist in the "flow" or motion of its components; a Heraclitean must also add that nothing ever persists in flowing in any particular way—for instance in "flowing white". Nothing persists, therefore, in any physical activity such that the effect of that activity upon the sensory activity of a normal percipient is the stable manifestation of a sense-property. If this is the case, then the equation of knowledge and perception is correct; for since the world consists of nothing whatsoever but disjointed events, there will be nothing for any man to know but those events which are sense-perceptions of his; so what I know is what I perceive, and what I perceive is what I know. For in such a world there is no point in reserving such notions as *truth* and *knowledge* for anything which is epistemologically on a higher level than awareness of immediate sense-experience, for in such a world there is nothing on a higher level than that. This seems to me to be roughly the position which Plato tries to meet.

He meets it by making the obvious point that such a world would be totally indescribable, and that if the doctrine is applied (as epistemologists so often forget to apply their

---

[1] Many students of Plato will entirely disagree with this account of the epistemology in the *Theaetetus*. For my reasons for thinking it correct see EPD 2, pp. 27–33.

doctrines) to the perceiving subject as well as to the world, there will be no such thing as perception. For the hypothesis that the word "perceive" has application to the world requires that there should exist certain stable and recurrent activities, namely seeing, hearing and the rest. Therefore, the assumption that there exist such states or activities as perceiving and knowing entails that there exists some stability on the side of the subject; and since perception must have objects, it entails also some stability on the side of the object. (One can of course perceive movement and change; but movement *of* something, change *in* something, and the something persists). Therefore we cannot use the formula that everything is in flux to justify the equation of knowledge with perception; we cannot argue that there exists nothing but perceptual events to be known. Knowledge is of stabilities, such as that this is, at the moment, white.

Plato seems to suggest that the proposition that *everything* is in flux was not much more than a debating stance. The sober truth that has been inflated into this absurd proposition, and that Plato accepts, is outlined by Socrates roughly as follows. Let there be, indeed, no "things"—nothing which is in its real nature completely changeless and inactive as this rock appears to be. Let the world consist of processes. Still we can divide the processes into two kinds, gradual and rapid. The gradual processes are what common sense call things, the rapid processes (or events) are the physical transactions which take place between them. The gradual processes can be divided into two kinds, "agents" and "patients" or objects and subjects. (An agent is a stimulator of sense-organs, a patient one whose sense-organs are stimulated. Clearly, as Socrates says, the difference between agents and patients is not ultimate; many objects that can be seen can also see). When a patient of a suitable kind comes into contact with an agent of a suitable kind (when a sentient being comes within range of a perceptible object) their intercourse begets twin offspring, namely two rapid events; in fact they interact. Plato does not commit himself to the form taken by these rapid events, except that he treats them as involving motion. From the *Timaeus* we could assume that in the case of sight they will be: the emission of light from the eyes and the emission of a "flame" of colour from the surface of the object, or the effect of these upon one another. However that may be (and Plato's account seems a little confused) their upshot is (where a man sees a rock, for example) that the man "becomes seeing" and the rock "becomes grey".

What Plato appears to think is that from an account such as this of how sense-perception takes place the Protagorean would go on to infer a phenomenalist doctrine of the physical world. If rocks as we know them in experience are grey, warm, hard, rough things; if all of these properties are sense-properties; and if sense-properties only exist as the correlates or "twins" of acts of perception; then the constituents of the physical world can only be "collections" as Plato calls them, or "families" as Price calls them, of these twins—of the momentary events whereby the rock, being seen, "becomes grey", being felt "becomes warm", and so on. And since no two perceptual transactions are ever precisely the same (for no two percipients, nor a single percipient on two occasions, are ever in precisely the same state), therefore there is no guarantee that one man's perceptions will agree with another's. What looks grey to me may seem khaki to you; what looks like a simple bedspread to me may swarm with pink rats to the drunkard. Therefore there is no public world, but only a series of private worlds—my world, consisting of my sense-perceptions, your world of yours, and so on. If these worlds to some extent correspond, well and good. But it cannot be guaranteed that there will be even rough correspondence, and it can be guaranteed that the correspondence will not be perfect.

In fact of course this account of how sense-perception takes place does not support a phenomenalist account of the world; one can only suppose it does if one forgets that the structure rests on the interaction between two physical processes. One cannot say: "Sense-data only arise when physical processes interact; therefore physical processes are only collections of sense-data." Nor does Plato want this account of sense-perception to support a phenomenalist epistemology. He wants it to support something more like the Causal Theory as we encounter it in, for example, Locke. According to this theory we need a distinction of levels of discourse which can be indicated by use of the phrases "the physical world" and "the empirical world". The physical world consists of Socrates' gradual processes. They are public; one rock can interact with many sentient organisms.

Primary qualities can be ascribed to its members; they occupy space, and therefore have size and shape, they stay still or move about. We can (though we need not) suppose its members to be built of particles in motion. But we cannot ascribe sense-properties to its members except in an indirect manner; the public physical rock can only be said to be grey if by that is meant that the effect of its physical interaction with the visual apparatus of a normal percipient under normal conditions will be the occurrence of a grey patch in that percipient's visual field. At another level, however, we can talk of the empirical world. Talking of the empirical world is talking of the world as common sense knows of it—a world consisting of things having sense-properties. This world of course is also public, for you normally can see the grey rock that I can see. But philosophical reflection can perhaps convince us that, when we talk about the members of this world, what we talk about can be regarded as collections of our own and other people's actual and possible sense-data. The rose as common sense knows of it consists of the views, smells and so on which are said to reveal it to us. Since your experiences and mine need not, perhaps do not, precisely correspond, the public empirical world can be said to be a sort of highest common factor of innumerable private empirical worlds which are sufficiently alike. At the empirical level, therefore, the private is ultimate; at the physical level this is not the case.

Plato does not distinguish between the physical level and the empirical (indeed he sometimes verbally confounds them), and he does not in so many words disentangle Phenomenalism from the Causal Theory. Indeed he suggests that the Protagoreans are right so far as immediate sense-experience is concerned, wrong only in so far as they overlook the fact that incorrigible statements, being reports of private perception, cannot claim the status of truths about the world. But in effect he does distinguish between Phenomenalism and the Causal Theory, allotting the former to his Protagorean-Heraclitean opponents and appropriating the latter for himself. For his rebuttal of his opponents does not simply depend upon the point that the (empirical) world must, if it is to be describable, be reasonably stable (so that even at this level there is more than just what-seems-to-me-now to be reported on—there is also what has been, is, and will be going on in public experience). It also

94

depends on the assumption that the degree of stability in the flux of sense-data which makes the empirical world describable derives from the fact that the behaviour of the physical processes whose interaction gives rise to sense-data is stable. It is only by ignoring this that you can become a Protagorean and suppose that I am in touch with nothing but my own private world.

Therefore, Plato's final account of sense-experience as we have it in the *Theaetetus* is along the following lines. Sense-data strictly speaking are not something cognitive; they are not atomic bits of knowing, they are occurrences. Specifically they are what happens when a bodily change, caused by interaction between the body and an external thing, is sufficiently intense to "penetrate through" to consciousness. (This strictly implies that we are conscious of, e.g. the physical changes in our eyes; we are not, and perhaps Plato should have said ". . . sufficiently intense to cause modifications in consciousness"). At any rate, such an occurrence is not a piece of information, it is merely an occurrence. We get no information until, at the very least, we notice the existence of the occurrence, and no information of any utility until we interpret its significance for the future course of our sense-experience. Information comes from calculations about what our senses undergo, not from the latter on their own. There is, therefore, an interaction in sense-experience between the senses and the mind. The senses contribute what Locke would have called ideas—of *grey* and *hot* and so on. But these are nothing to us until the mind brings to the interpretations of them concepts of its own which it does not get from experience —*existence*, *similarity* and the like.[1] In themselves the senses are independent of each other, sight related only to coloured

[1] Those who dislike the notion that the mind contributes concepts like *similarity* and *existence* out of its own resources can perhaps help themselves to swallow it by thinking of it in the following way. To notice that A resembles B we must have compared them. To notice the existence of C we must have in some sense isolated it, objectified it, disentangled it from the subject-self. But these activities of comparing and isolating, which are, as it were, applications of the concepts of *similarity* and *existence*, are not activities which the mind can learn from experience. For we cannot *have* experience, in the sense of something from which we can learn, until we have already begun to compare and isolate. There is no mind until there is something that can compare and isolate, and no objective world until these activities are exercised upon the given. In this sense *existence* and *similarity* are concepts which the mind contributes to experience (In the form in which I have presented it, this argument is of course more reminiscent of Kant than of Plato. But it is not inconceivable that Plato may have had thoughts which went roughly along these lines).

expanses, hearing to sounds. We therefore get no contact with reality through the senses in themselves, but only through the mental activity whereby the occurrences in the senses are observed, collated and compared. To suppose that our eyes and ears tell us things is to treat our eyes and ears as scouts, ourselves as the headquarters to which the scouts report. *We* tell things, by observing what goes on in our eyes and ears and interpreting its significance.

Socrates concludes this part of the discussion by the remark that knowledge is not to be looked for in the sphere of sensation but in the sphere of "properly mental activity" about the world; this is, he says, the sphere of what we call *doxa*, belief, opinion or judgment. The *Theaetetus* then proceeds to discuss whether knowledge can be defined as true belief, an equation which it fails to find a satisfactory sense for. Accordingly we do not know whether Socrates would allow that there can strictly speaking be such a thing as knowledge (*epistêmê*) of the empirical world; all he tells us is that sensation by itself cannot provide it, since it cannot provide us with true beliefs.

7

Knowledge and Belief

THE question of the relationship between knowledge and true belief (or right belief, for Plato sometimes seems to avoid the honorific word *alêthês* or "true" in this context) is one which often arises in the dialogues. That there are two distinct states, knowledge and true belief, seems to be taken for granted throughout; it is their relationship which is problematical. Some of these discussions are simple, some very intricate. I shall try to give what seems to me to be the essential problem that Plato was concerned with.

In this connection we need to clear our minds of two ideas. One is familiar to us from recent discussions of knowledge and belief, namely that the difference between them lies essentially in the goodness or badness of our grounds—that well-grounded true beliefs count as knowledge, those which are less well grounded are merely belief. This may, perhaps, get the demarcation-line in the right place, but it involves seeing the question from the wrong angle. The other is the text-book doctrine that for Plato the sphere of knowledge is forms or *a priori* truths, and the sphere of belief is matters of empirical fact. This seems to me partially false, and totally misleading. It is partially false because Plato allows both that there can be beliefs about forms (indeed when the *Republic* talks about beliefs it is almost exclusively concerned with beliefs about forms), and also that there can be knowledge of matters which are certainly not *a priori* truths; for example a local inhabitant can know the way to Beachy Head, and the user of an implement can know what it ought to be like.

We need to start by thinking of two opposite poles. They can be called knowing and not knowing if the first is thought of as the absolute grasp of something, the second the condition of being totally out of touch with it. Plato was convinced of the obvious truth that there is a spectrum of intermediate conditions in between these two extremes. Socrates in the *Symposium* compares the relationship between the two poles to that between beauty and ugliness; what lacks the one does not necessarily possess the other. In jargon, they are contraries, not contradictories. This seems obvious enough; Plato's problem was to discover how to assert this obvious truth without becoming entangled in contradictions. But why should there be any risk of this? Perhaps the following argument will bring the point out as well as any other.

Take some topic such as justice, and some man, say Cephalus. Let us suppose that Cephalus has, as we might want to say, some grasp of the nature of justice. He is not, therefore, ignorant of it, as Romulus might be if the wolf never told him of it, or as Callicles might be if he thought that justice was that the strong should inherit the earth. But do we want to say that Cephalus knows justice? Hardly, for when Socrates asks him to define it, he excuses himself and leaves the discussion. But justice is an intelligible principle in accordance with which we sort men and actions into sheep and goats. A man cannot be said to have grasped justice until he can give an account of the principle in accordance with which this sorting is done, or in other words until he has reactivated an explicit understanding of the *rationale* of certain civilized procedures. Cephalus has not achieved this, and, therefore, he has not grasped justice. But on this topic his mind is not empty. It has, therefore, grasped something. But what it has grasped is not justice; it must, therefore, be something else. But if what is in Cephalus' mind on the subject of justice is not justice, but something else, then Cephalus is out of touch with justice; he is, therefore, ignorant of it after all.

Mutatis mutandis the same can be done with the road to Beachy Head. The man who knows the road to Beachy Head has that road on call in his mind, as the local inhabitant has it. But this cannot be said of many people who can nevertheless give you correct directions how to get from here to there. Such persons have something in their minds, but it is not the road to Beachy Head; therefore, what they have in their minds is not

98

the road to Beachy Head; therefore they are ignorant of it. Generally speaking, if we want to say of some man that he is neither fully knowledgeable of some topic A nor totally out of touch with it, we shall have to say that what he has in his mind is not A but something else; for if he had A in his mind he would be fully knowledgeable about A. But if what he has in his mind is something other than A, it follows that he is not in touch with A. Therefore, there can be no states between knowledge and ignorance.

A mental state which consists in being neither in nor out of touch with A would seem to demand as its content something which neither is nor is not A. If the content of the state were A itself, then the state would be knowledge; if the content of the state were definitely not A, then the state would be ignorance of A. When Plato first introduces the topic of knowledge and belief in the *Republic* he uses riddling language rather like this. He argues that when a man has a belief he has something. But what he has cannot be the thing itself about which the belief is. If it were, how could you differentiate between knowledge and belief? Yet they are clearly different for the one is infallible and the other is not. But what the believer has in his mind, being something, cannot be a non-entity, as is the case in the state of ignorance. Therefore, it must be something between reality and non-entity. What is there, however, which occupies this mysterious position? Socrates tells us that conventional opinions about such things as beauty do so. For conventional opinions about beauty represent it as "many beauties", or "many beautifuls". The plain man, that is to say, says that beauty is bold colouring, and symmetry and delicacy and this and that. Since none of these "many beauties" is always beautiful—since each of them indeed is sometimes ugly—conventional opinions about beauty are seriously but not totally misguided. Therefore, that which is encapsulated in such opinions is not beauty itself; on the other hand it is not a non-entity as it would be if it were either nothing, or something totally other than beauty, pretending to be this. The content of such opinions, therefore, is neither reality nor non-entity, and therefore such opinions are fit objects of a mental state which is neither knowledge nor ignorance.[1]

[1] This is not the traditional interpretation of the passage at the end of *Republic* 5. See EPD 2, pp. 53–69.

Later in the same dialogue where Plato wishes to discuss how we can progress from ignorance towards knowledge, and where therefore he wishes to show that there are many gradations between the two end-points, he does so by making use of the notion of an image, an entity such as a shadow, reflection or echo. An image is something of ambiguous value. If it is mistaken for a reality it can do considerable harm; if it is recognized to be an image it can be of assistance. If I cannot see Queen Victoria I can get guidance as to her appearance from a statue; if I cannot see my own face, I can look at its replica in the polished panels of my car. For an image is something which owes certain of its properties (its shape, probably, and perhaps its colour) to the appropriate properties of its original.

It does not require much divination to see how the parallel is to be applied. For the plain man's conventional account of beauty, if he is a sensible plain man, owes its general outlines to the fact that beauty is what it is. That is what makes an account of something a sound account, namely that it is determined by the reality to which it relates. Plato therefore starts by calling our attention to the relationship between the confidence that we are entitled to have when we have something before our eyes and the conjecture to which we are reduced when all we have to go upon is a shadow or reflection; and in two elaborate—over-elaborate—figures he argues that the same relationship obtains between other terms. He supposes that we all start down in a cavern, interested only in appearances. He includes in this, no doubt, the actual appearances of physical things, but he intends primarily to say that the natural condition of human boorishness is one of being concerned only with moral appearances. The totally ignorant, that is to say, cannot tell a right act from a wrong one, being indefinitely deceivable by specious claims. Nor can he tell a good table from a bad one, since all he knows of a table is what it looks like. From these base beginnings we can be forced to progress to a condition in which we can distingusish concrete instances of right from those of wrong, and in which likewise we can tell good tables from bad ones, having learnt to judge between them technologically rather than by looks. In this progression we pass from images to realities, in the sense that the relationship between the later state and the earlier is the same as the relationship between direct confrontation with something, and confrontation with it only *via* an image of it. The same relationship obtains, when we are considering the study of abstract principles, between concerning ourselves with a principle directly and concerning ourselves only with its concrete instances; the instances are an image of the principle in that, as we saw, the fact that these and these are, more or less, what justice amounts to in terms of concrete instances is something which is due to the nature of justice as an abstract principle. Its instances are not it; but if it were different, its instances would be different. In passing from concern with instances to concern with principles we pass from the sphere of belief to the sphere of knowledge. The reason for this language is perhaps that so long as we confine ourselves to concern with instances of, say, justice, our state of mind with respect to justice cannot be more than belief. When we try to concern ourselves with principles in themselves, we must progress from what we cannot ever fully understand towards what, in theory we can; for one only "understands" instances in the light of principles. The technique which Plato puts forward in this part of the *Republic* for beginning the philosophic study of principles is the study of mathematics. The idea seems to be that mathematics is an abstract discipline in which everything is ignored but quantitative and spatial relationships. Therefore the mathematical embodiments of abstract principles are especially clear, if only because of the lack of distractions in the subject-matter. The concept of equality has application both in politics and in mathematics. If we want to understand what equality is, and whether or not it has diverse forms, we shall find it easier to consider these matters in the dispassionate field of mathematics than in the passionate field of politics. But the study of mathematics would be of no use to the student of abstract rational principles if it were not the case that mathematical order is the fruit of the application of these principles to the field of space and number. The student of mathematics, therefore, is studying images of the forms, and the contrast between direct confrontation, and confrontation *via* an image applies to the contrast between the student of mathematics and the dialectician or philosopher. For the latter is at least trying to achieve direct confrontation with the principles whose embodiments in space and number the former is familiar with. The mathematician can of course, like anyone else who has an image before him, fail to recognize it as an image. He can suppose that he is confronted with an original. He can fail to ask, for example, what a number is, contenting himself with an intuitive, sensuous representation of it as, say, a group of pips like those on a playing-card. If he does this he will fail to begin to philosophize, and he will miss the significance of his study as one that comprises the clearest possible embodiments of abstract principles.

All this is very complicated, but the effect of it can be represented thus. If we take some topic such as, once more, justice, we can find more than one condition of mind in between the extremes of knowing justice and being ignorant of it. Knowing justice is something which, perhaps, nobody has achieved; it would mean understanding the intelligible principle which justifies differentiating the just from the unjust. Being ignorant of justice is something that we all start from, and rest in, except in so far as we are somehow forced to do better. It means being guided in our application of the labels "just" and "unjust" only by the appearances[1] of the men or actions we apply them to, and not at all by the reality of them. Above this, at the top of the sphere of belief, is the condition of being able to tell an instance of justice from an instance of injustice, getting it right on almost every occasion. The bottom of the sphere of intelligence (the bottom of the staircase leading to knowledge) is in one way level with, in another way superior to, the top of the sphere of belief; it is the familiarity with justice in whatever embodiments this principle has in the field of mathematics, and also perhaps in those realms of nature (astronomy and music) which the study of mathematics opens to us. Above this, of course, comes the apprehension of the principle in itself, apart from any embodiment.

The details of all this (the details of the interpretation of the "similes" of the Line and Cave) are complex and contentious. But it is fairly clear that the Cave wants to say that there are stages in between being so ignorant of justice that we can only divide the just from the unjust by appearances, and, at the other end of the scale, really knowing and understanding the abstract principle underlying our propensity to make this division—an

---

[1] Or "reputes"; a reputation is an appearance in Greek.

achievement incidentally which involves an equal understanding of all other principles in the light of their source, the nature of goodness. It is clear also that Plato's answer to the question how it is possible to be not totally out of touch with some reality is that we do this by apprehending an image of that reality.

It will be well to recollect at this point that the idea that one can be not totally out of touch with some reality which, however, one has not yet grasped, is an idea which is of vital importance to Plato. For, as we have seen, his whole understanding of philosophy is that what the philosopher tries to do is to achieve an explicit insight into the *rationale* of the intellectual moves which he every day makes as a thinking being. One could never come to understand that which one was totally out of touch with at the beginning. As the myth in the *Phaedrus* puts it, no soul can animate a human body unless it has had some glimpses of the forms in the discarnate condition. Many souls have had a poor view and have seen only a few forms; and these no doubt become stupid and gullible men. But without some pre-natal vision of a form a man would be unable to "unify in thought what is presented in manifold sense-experiences"; in fact he would be unable to conceptualize. Therefore, the ignorance from which we start is not total and absolute ignorance. Or rather, as the *Sophist* suggests (229 e), the condition from which we start becomes total ignorance only if we allow it to become an absolute barrier to apprehending the truth by supposing ourselves to know when we do not. A man puts himself out of touch with some reality by identifying his image of it with the reality itself. My idea of justice is not absolutely false; that belongs to my idea that my idea of justice is justice. Socrates was the wisest man in Greece because he alone knew that he was a fool.

It is clear also that this passage is not primarily concerned to say that we cannot have knowledge of matters of fact. Plato is concerned to plot the epistemological status of my belief that justice is telling the truth, paying debts and so on; this is not knowledge because it involves my possessing only an image of the reality I am speaking of. He is not concerned to plot the epistemological status of my belief that Waterloo was fought in 1815.

H

Knowledge and Belief

One thing that is not clear is whether Plato felt bound to say that the image, which is grasped by a man who is not totally out of touch with some reality, must exist *in rerum natura*; or is it enough that it exists in the mind? Did he think that whatever has to be mentioned in epistemological analysis must have some sort of objective existence? Such views have been maintained in living memory (consider the doctrine of propositions demolished by Ryle in the *Proceedings* of the Aristotelian Society for 1929–30); and holding such views is commonly called "Platonism". Was Plato a "Platonist"? Certainly as we have seen he sometimes wrote as if he thought that the world of vulgar common sense was identical with the physical world, as if common-sense hardness, which is compatible with softness, was a property of material things. For myself I doubt whether he did think this. Certainly none of his arguments seem to depend on it, and at least one depends on its contradictory. Moreover, if I had to concede that at the time of the *Republic* Plato would have said that vulgar hardness is an objectively existing image of true hardness, I should still contend that I saw no evidence for thinking that this delusion persisted.

So far the relation between knowledge and belief is that when I know I grasp some reality, and when I have sound belief I grasp, or have in my mind, something which Plato likens to an image of that reality. In the context of the knowledge of rational principles (which is what Plato is concerned with in the *Republic*), we get these images by doing what he would describe as paying attention to the deliverances of the senses. A man has an image of beauty, more or less sound, if he applies this concept, with more or less discrimination, but without full understanding, to concrete cases. In that case he has a conception of beauty, but the conception is not theoretical. In the last resort it has the form *that A things and B things and C things are beautiful* (where A, B and C are the evident features of various sets of beautiful things—symmetry for example and bold colouring). It is therefore a conception of beauty in terms of the many beauties. Such an image turns into an idol if we suppose it to be the original; it can be used as a base for further meditation if we avoid this supposition. It is in this light that we should understand Plato's attacks on the intrusion of "the senses" into philosophy. He means that you must not allow what you get from your eyes and ears with only a small critical contribution from the mind to masquerade as understanding; for if you do you will cut yourself off from knowledge.

Does he, however, want to say that there can be no knowledge of mundane things, in the consideration of which we could surely persuade him that the evidence of the senses is very important? Does he want to deny that the contrast between knowledge and belief has application in this sphere? The answer seems to be that he does sometimes say explicitly and seriously that the contrast does apply. He allows that the native can know the way to somewhere, the eye-witness know what happened, the user of an implement know what it ought to be like;[1] and he contrasts such knowledge with the right belief that is the most that one can achieve through being correctly informed. On the other hand there are other places where he takes it for granted that we cannot strictly know mundane truths. It is possible to argue, however, that in these places he is primarily thinking of general scientific truths, for example about the orbit of the moon, and that it may be that the explanation of this scepticism is nothing more profound than the absence in Plato's time of reliable methods of collecting the necessary information. In the absence of this, science must be, as the *Timaeus* stresses, a body of conjecture, the only certitudes in it being those which tell us about the considerations to which the creative reason, being rational, must have attached weight.

But it could be asked whether a contrast between knowledge and belief in mundane matters could possibly be at all like a contrast between knowledge and belief in the sphere of rational principles. The answer is that it could; and it will be illuminating to see why. Knowledge for Plato is the intellectual possession of an object; what I know is part of me and also part of the objective world. Now the only way in which I can achieve intellectual possession of a man, a place, an event or something of the kind is through intimate acquaintance with it. I must be familiar with the man, live in the place, have witnessed the event. And with regard to that man, for example, I cannot get beyond this. With regard to his humanity or other general characteristics there is of course progress in understanding to be made; but with regard to his individuality I cannot get beyond

---

1 *Meno* 97, *Theaetetus* 201, and *Republic* 601–2 respectively.

what familiar acquaintance gives me, for there *is* nothing beyond. What makes you not just a man, but *you*, is your being the person you are; and this I can only become familiar with.[1] Therefore, in the scale of knowing you there is nothing beyond intimate acquaintance, and no reason to withhold the title "knowledge" from this in order to bestow it elsewhere. In contrast with this state of *bien connaître*, we have various grades of *savoir*, of knowing *that*—knowing that you are bald, without acquaintance with your individual baldness, that you are witty without acquaintance with the individual savour of your wit, and so on. What I possess when I *know-that* many things about you, but do not *know you*, could even, if we wished, be described as an image of you. It is a bit like having a map of a piece of country I have never visited; and a map is an image in a fairly obvious sense. Therefore, the contrast between knowing and believing, being the contrast between intellectual possession of something and intellectual possession of an image or surrogate of it, can be applied in the realm of mundane objects as in the realm of rational principles, and is very much the same contrast in the two realms. On the other hand the question can be raised whether I can strictly have intellectual possession of a mundane object as I can of an intelligible principle; or even whether a mundane object is strictly an objective reality. The tree by my garden gate with which I am so familiar grows in the garden, and not in my mind, a contrast which could not be applied to triangularity if I really knew what this was. And the tree is after all in the last analysis only some pattern in a physical flux. Its individuality therefore vanishes into space (which is opaque to intelligence)[2] characterized by certain general terms. There cannot, therefore, strictly be intellectual possession of the individuality of an individual thing or event, but only of the general features which it shares with many others. Individuals, therefore, are not strictly intelligible entities, and for that reason there cannot strictly be knowledge of them. One can contrast the optimum apprehension of an individual, through personal acquaintance, with the apprehension of it only through correct information as to its general features; and one can liken this contrast to that between knowledge and belief in the sphere of general principles. But perhaps one ought to say that strictly

[1] Cp. *Theaetetus* 209.   [2] *Timaeus* 52 b, EPD 2, p. 217.

speaking even optimum acquaintance with individuals is not intellectual possession of an objective reality and cannot therefore count as knowledge, though it does stand to something below it in the relationship in which knowledge stands to belief. I do not know whether Plato ever pursued such a train of thought as this; but if he did, that would explain both why he sometimes speaks seriously of knowledge of mundane individuals, and also why he sometimes speaks as if there could not be such a thing.

8

The Logic of Knowing and Believing

WE were unable to decide whether Plato thought there could, strictly speaking, be knowledge of mundane individuals. However, it does seem to be possible to assert that the discussion of knowledge and belief in the second half of the *Theaetetus* represents a tussle in Plato's mind over the relationship between *connaître* and *savoir*, over the relationship between knowledge of individuals and knowledge of general truths. It is not possible to be sure what the tussle was; the point of much of the argument is obscure. One thing that Plato is certainly bringing out is that there must be grades of acquaintance; a point which raises, but does not settle, the question which of them can count as knowledge. There is a long discussion of mistakes which centres around the proposition that it is impossible to make a mistake about anything, because either you do not know it, in which case nothing you say can relate to it, or you do know it in which case you cannot get it wrong. Socrates seems to try to bring out in various ways that it is possible to be sufficiently in touch with something to be able to refer to it, yet not so intimately acquainted with it that one must be infallible about it. This Socrates does in terms of the knowledge of persons. Admitting that I cannot mistake Jones for Robinson if I have never heard of Robinson, nor Jones for anyone at all if I know Jones well and have a clear view of him, he shows that there are various ways in which I can mistake Jones for Robinson if I know Robinson. The philosophical value of this rather obvious point is that there are grades of acquaintance.

Socrates then proceeds to get into difficulties about how we can make mistakes, not in identifying something we can see, but in abstract matters such as arithmetic. His arguments seem to suggest that we must distinguish being familiar with a number from knowing everything about it. One who does not know the numbers 7 and 5 cannot count; but a man who can count, and therefore knows these numbers, can still think that $7+5=11$. But if knowing 7 and 5 meant knowing them as the numbers whose sum is 12, we could not make such a mistake. Perhaps the conclusion that this points to is along these lines: I cannot *fully* "know" the number 12 unless I know it as the sum of 7 and 5; but I can still "know" 12 well enough to use the numeral intelligently though I suppose it to be the sum of 7 and 6. In this case I cannot be said to be fully in touch with the reality in question—the number 12—though I am not totally out of touch with it. I know (*savoir*) a selection of facts about it; but I evidently do not fully know (*connaître*) the reality itself. In such a case I retain touch with the number 12 by having in my mind, not the number itself, but a representation or impression of it—to wit certain facts about it. Is there, then, a kind of knowing which involves the possession not of the reality itself, but of a representation of it? Worse still, is there perhaps no such thing as direct acquaintance with an abstract entity such as a number?

This would have worried Plato. For years he had used *connaître*-language about the knowledge of abstract matters. Phrases like "knowing the triangle", or "knowing the triangle, what it is" (parallel to "I know thee who thou art") are common in such writings as the *Republic*. Unkind interpreters are inclined to say that of course Plato talked about knowing the triangle, because the triangle, or any other form, was an individual substance and knowing it was having a sort of vision by which you got acquainted with it. And they have it on their side that Plato does indeed use a good deal of vision-language and acquaintance-language about the knowledge of forms. But there is no need to take such language too seriously; and even if one does take it seriously there is no need to put this interpretation upon it. (The interpretation gets grotesque when Plato says that good carpenters look towards the form of table before making a table. Carpenters do not have trances and visions in such a situation, but they do ask themselves questions which could be expressed in the formula "What does being a table consist in?"). For if we suppose that Plato did not think that phrases like "knowing the triangle" involved a metaphorical use of the *connaître*-sense of "know", it does not follow that he thought that they did not. We distinguish uncles from aunts, but we use "cousin" for both sexes. We should not, however, be accused of believing that female cousins are male; we just do not think it useful to distinguish. Plato likewise may well have failed to notice that knowing Theaetetus was very unlike knowing justice, without therefore thinking that the two were very alike. I think it is very probable that the second half of the *Theaetetus* is a product of the birth-pangs of the recognition that the two are rather unlike, but I do not think he had previously thought the opposite. He just had not thought.

There is one theme, introduced in the *Theaetetus* and developed in its sequel the *Sophist*, which is relevant to this. This is the theme of the importance of the notion of a *that*-clause or proposition in the analysis of belief. It seems to me not clear whether Plato ever allowed that propositions are important in the analysis of knowledge. I suspect that he always hankered after a *connaître*-analysis of knowledge, at any rate in the case of knowledge of forms, but *not* for the reason that he thought forms to be individual substances. Rather I suspect (and all this is pretty rank guess-work, supported a little by a passage in the Seventh Letter)[1] that he would have wanted to preserve phrases like "knowing circularity" on the ground that *understanding* circularity must always go beyond knowing *that* a circle is this or that. It must also, for example, involve knowing *how* to understand any true statement about a circle, knowing how to meet any objection which can be brought against it, and so on. Really to understand an abstract principle is to have one's mind fully informed by it. This involves knowing all the true propositions that relate to it, but it goes beyond this rather in the way in which knowing London goes beyond knowing innumerable true propositions. It is *because* he knows London that a taxi-driver can answer your questions correctly; no number of correct answers could exhaust his knowledge.

But that *that*-clauses are essential to the analysis of belief is

---

[1] Ep. 7, 342–4, EPD 2, pp. 122 sqq.

certainly a theme of these dialogues—though not of course in anything like these words. To see the significance of this—one of Plato's greatest contributions to our understanding of the logic of our discourse—we must retreat and approach it from a distance.

We saw earlier that, though it could be argued that there was nothing in between knowledge and ignorance, still Plato took it as obvious that there was such an intermediary. We saw also that he used the notion of an image to elucidate how this could be. But there is an argument in the *Sophist* which shows that the notion of an image is a lame duck in this context. For an image is essentially something which is not what it purports to be; therefore, an image is essentially something that is not; therefore there are no images—for everything is what it *is*, and being an image is not being something. Anything that you feel tempted to call an image should in fact be called a something else. So having in one's mind an image of X would just be, once more, not having X in one's mind but something different. So there can be nothing in between knowledge and ignorance. What you have in your mind is what you have in your mind, and if that is not X, then X is not in your mind, and you are not in touch with it. Trying to say that you are in touch with it "to some extent" is using a mere bromide. In his earlier years Plato seems to have felt that you need not trouble with arguments which lead to silly conclusions—just as he sometimes acted as if you need not trouble too much about the logical rigour of arguments which lead to sound ones; as he grew older his conscience seems to have become more tender. Parallels with shadows and reflections would no longer suffice, therefore, to explain how one can be neither in touch with something nor yet out of touch with it. "That's a bit free and easy, isn't it?", as Parmenides says to Socrates when he uses an analogy, having been asked for an analysis.

We can see what the fundamental trouble is if we revert to the argument about knowledge and belief at the end of the fifth book of the *Republic*. It was like skating on thin ice between Scylla and Charybdis trying to give the gist of that argument without either stripping it of all apparent cogency or showing how the trick is worked. The argument involved the step that *doxa* (by which in this context Plato means something like

"having an impression of"—i.e. having a not altogether unsound opinion) cannot be the same thing as ignorance, because
what corresponds to *doxa* is something which is, whereas what
corresponds to ignorance is something which is-not, a non-
entity. But what does Socrates mean when he makes non-
entities correspond to ignorance? What he has in mind seems
to be something like having a totally false idea of some topic.
But then in that case a non-entity—a totally false idea—is not
nothing, but something. Therefore the distinction between
doxa, or *having an impression of*, and *ignorance* vanishes. One
cannot either have an impression of something, or totally
traduce it, without having something in one's mind. We could
of course reintroduce the distinction by saying that in the one
case the something is something partly true, whereas in the
other case it is something false. But Plato is operating in this
passage without the notions of truth and falsehood, relying
instead on those of being and not being.

To ask why he is doing this is to begin to see the point. When
it is raining, and I say that it is, what do I report? Obviously
something that is, a fact, a constituent of the world. When it is
not raining, and I say that it is, what do I report? Certainly not
something that is. But I do not just not report; I report something, and therefore something that is-not—the rain which is
not happening. Common sense says that of course there can be
false beliefs and false statements. But the Eleatics had a variety
of arguments to show that there cannot be (that from the
Theaetetus about the impossibility of mistakes being among
them). For an Eleatic would say that the rain that is not
happening is of course not an existent non-entity—there is just
no such thing. When I wrongly said that it was raining, therefore, I did not report a non-entity; I reported nothing, and,
since there is no such thing as nothing, I did not report or say
anything at all.

How did we get into this tangle? In something like the following way. "Report", and certain other verbs of *saying* such as
"mention" or "recount", can govern either a direct object or a
that-clause. (Plato shows his awareness of this by the tricks he
plays with *legein* in *Euthydemus* 283–4). In the direct-object
construction what is reported is a constituent of the world,
existent or non-existent; in the other construction what is

reported is a proposition, true or false. The temptation to say that when I make a false statement I say nothing arises from confusing the two objects. The rain that is not happening is a non-existent situation. Therefore, when I falsely say that it is raining what I report in the direct-object construction is non-existent. But of course I still report or convey something in the other construction—I convey the proposition that it is raining. The puzzle can only be got rid of if we see that there is some proposition that I assert (though it is false), but no situation such that if it existed it would make my proposition true. It is by transferring the predicate "non-existent" from the situation which I allege to the proposition in which I allege it that one produces the impression that I allege something which is non-existent and therefore nothing. It is in fact by leaving the proposition out of the analysis, and concentrating on the situation, that the trouble arises.

The reason for leaving the proposition out is obvious enough; it comes from starting from the end of truth. It is so easy to say that when I know something what I grasp with my mind is an actual piece of the external world, and that when I make a true remark what I report is the same. Generally speaking I know or say something that is. "Something that is", therefore, can very easily come to have the flavour of "true", especially in Greek where the verb for *to be* tends to connote *really being*. There seems to be no need to intrude a proposition between the knower or speaker and that which he knows or reports on. It is only when what he thinks or says is not in fact part of the objective world that this causes trouble. We are tempted in these cases to say that the man thinks or says something that is not, both because this is the opposite of "something that is", and also because the situation that the man alleges does not in fact exist. The device whereby we avoid giving the impression that in the case of falsehood what is said is non-existent, is to introduce the concept of a proposition—thus generating new problems about the relationship between propositions and the world.

Plato was aware of the problems concerning non-existence. He brings out in an argument in the *Parmenides* that if you mention something you must mention it as existent, and that, therefore, the analysis of anything of the form "Fairies are non-existent" must be complex; one cannot be attributing to fairies the predicate of non-existence. In the *Sophist* he offers an analysis of negation in terms of difference. He explains that "A is not B" is to be taken as "A is something other than B." This, however, will not suffice for "A is not an existent"; for if A is something other than any existent, then there is no such thing as A, and we still do not know how we succeeded in mentioning it. Therefore, the analysis of negation in terms of *being other than* will not deal with the problem of the man who alleges something non-existent; he still, it seems, alleges nothing. Plato sees this, and, though he does not deal with the question how to analyse existence-denials in general, he deals with the problem of how one can say that somebody has alleged something non-existent by, in effect, introducing the notion of the proposition, or, perhaps it would be better to say, by improving the current understanding of what a proposition is. (This is not to say that he distinguishes, as we did above, between the proposition, which is false, and the alleged situation, which is non-existent, in a case of false statement—partly, no doubt, because this still leaves us with the problem of non-existence).

It is, I suppose, a natural theory of discourse to treat a sentence as being the same thing as a word, only longer. If I say "tree" I mention a tree; if I say "palm-tree" I narrow my reference to a certain kind of tree; if I say "monkey up palm-tree" I narrow it further to a tree of that kind embellished with a monkey. Pidgin manages to communicate with strings of words like "monkey up palm-tree" which lack a verb, and it is natural to think that there is no important differences between this and "There is a monkey up that palm-tree." Nor is there of course, so long as convention decrees that the asserting function, which is normally discharged by the verb, is to be somehow understood. In the absence of this convention a verb-less phrase will, however, function in some ways as a single word functions; it may for example be capable of denoting, and it will be incapable of asserting. (We commonly form single words to abbreviate verb-less phrases—"insecticide" for "substance lethal to insects"). If, however, a sentence is thought to be merely an example of a phrase of this kind trouble will arise. Once again it arises over falsehood. Just as "Trafalgar Square" can be thought to be the name of a London district, so "There's a monkey up that palm-tree" can be thought to name a different sort of component of the world, namely the fact that there is a monkey up that palm-tree—but only if, as a matter of fact, there is. If there is no monkey up the palm-tree, then "There's a monkey up that palm-tree" names nothing; and since (we are supposing) sentences are a kind of long name, the sentence must be meaningless. This conveniently reinforces the argument that one cannot meaningfully call a proposition false (for such a proposition would have asserted something non-existent, and therefore nothing) by showing that utterances can be divided into those which name components of the world and are, therefore, meaningful and true, and those which do not name anything and are therefore not false but meaningless—not even names, but mere sounds.

The trouble of course arises firstly from treating all words as names, secondly from supposing that sentences are long words. In the *Theaetetus* Socrates relates a theory which he claims to have heard in a dream which argues that one cannot make a statement about a simple, uncompounded entity, on the ground that every statement must contain a complex of elements and must therefore be the name of the complex of entities named by its components. No statement, therefore, can "belong to" just one simple entity. The theory contains further complications, and Socrates shows it to be inconsistent without telling us which parts of it he wants to keep and which to reject. If we could assume that he thought it was in fact possible to make a statement about a simple entity, we could argue that he had offered us a *reductio ad absurdum* of the view that a statement is a name. The Greek for "simple entity" or "element" is the same as the Greek for "letter of the alphabet", and Socrates certainly succeeds in making statements about letters in this context. It is possible, however, that he would have preferred to say that he was giving us a *reductio ad absurdum* of the notion that there could be a simple entity; if *S*, he might say, was just *S* and not also a letter (and therefore something compound), then we could not truly say: "*S* is a letter". However this may be, the Eleatic Stranger in the *Sophist* unquestionably makes the point that statements are not names. Every statement, he says, must consist of what he calls "a name" and of "something said". (The words that he uses became technical terms for "noun" and "verb"). Of these elements the first carries the referring function, the second the asserting function. This deals with the problem of false belief and false statement in the following way. When I falsely say that Jones is drunk I name something real (Jones) and ascribe to it something real (drunkenness). I do not either name or assert the non-existent Jones'-drunkenness. What differentiates truth from falsity is simply that in the latter case the reality that I ascribe is other than any of those which characterize the reality to which I ascribe it, whereas in the former case, that of truth, the ascribed reality is among those which do belong to the subject to whom it is ascribed. We are dealing throughout with existent things—existent subjects and existent predicates—and with the two relations *being identical with one of the predicates which belong to* (P has this relation to S when it is true that S is P), and *being other than any of the predicates which belong to* (the relation of P to S when it is false that S is P). Non-existence and negativity do not come into the story at all, neither when we are analysing "S is not P" nor when we are analysing "It is false that S is P." We manage with *l'être* and dispense with *le néant.* The importance of this goes of course a good way beyond the particular paradox of false belief that it was introduced to deal with. The doctrine that every meaningful statement contains a "name" and "something said", that no statement is just a string of words, is the ancestor of the doctrine of subject and predicate as we find it in Aristotle (and indeed of the doctrine of referring as we find it in Strawson); and the treatment of negation, incomplete though it is, is sufficient to have disposed in advance of "Platonistic" theories according to which there must in some sense exist worlds to accommodate the quasi-facts reported by false statements. False statements do not have to tell us about subsistent realms of unactualized possibility; as the *Theaetetus* adumbrated, we can deal with mistakes in terms of mis-distribution of the contents of the actual world in the mind of the person who makes the mistake.

The relevance of this to the question of the relationship between knowledge and belief is that, at any rate at the level of saying that Jones is drunk or that $7+5=12$, we cannot, so to speak, use the grammar of *connaître.* We cannot treat the object of the verb "to say" or "to believe" as a sort of individual—as Jones'-drunkenness-now, if that is conceived of as the sort of thing we could be acquainted with in the way we can be acquainted with Jones. What we have in mind when we believe that Jones is drunk is not Jones-drunkenness-now, but the proposition *that Jones is drunk*. We have to say this, or at any rate it is wise to say this, even in the case of true belief, for the reason that otherwise we shall be tempted to say that we have nothing in mind when our belief is false, when Jones is not in fact drunk, and when therefore there is no such thing as Jones'-drunkenness-now.

This seems to be among the problems active in Plato's mind when he discusses the relation between belief and knowledge in the *Theaetetus*. There are one or two places in the course of the argument where the notion of a *that*-clause seems to be pointed towards—places at any rate where the use of it would get Socrates out of pits which he digs for himself. But the discussion is too inconclusive to allow one to say what position Plato had come to.

Why indeed should one say that he had come to any conclusion? He need not have solved all the problems that he thought of. Possibly, however, we can find various clues as to the sort of doctrine he might have sympathized with. The *Theaetetus* mingles discussion of the knowledge of abstract matters (of arithmetical truths, of what a waggon is) with discussion of the knowledge of individuals. The passage in the Seventh Letter mentioned above seems to say that to know something such as circularity in the fullest sense is to have gone beyond the ability to define or use the concept, to a stage which can only be metaphorically described in terms of the breaking out of light. Taking these together one may wonder whether Plato thought that knowledge of abstract matters was to be likened to the knowledge of an individual (not because abstract matters were some kind of transcendent individual, but because no set of true statements could ever exhaust the content of such knowledge), and that anything that consisted merely in the ability to make true statements was always by comparison a state of *doxa*, because it did not involve the absolute identification of oneself with the reality in question.

This ought to be taken in conjunction with what we have said throughout was Plato's conception of the nature and goal of philosophy. We engage in philosophy because we are intelligences, though intelligences which see in a glass darkly because we are forced to give our attention primarily to the evident, pragmatically important features of things. The smell, for example, of onions, being essentially a trivial by-product of their mode of functioning, has a disproportionate importance in our conception of them. The goal of philosophy is to become so far as possible pure intelligences, in the way perhaps in which the stars are almost that, they being things which simply conform in their bodily movements to the demands of reason. Is it not possible in this frame of mind to conceive of what has to be formulated in discrete propositions as no more than a half-way house on the way to a stage at which one's apprehension of the world simply is the all-inclusive *totum simul* vision of creative reason which is reponsible for the order of the world? It would be optimistic perhaps to hope to achieve this vision, but there is no reason to believe Plato thought that knowledge in the fullest sense had ever been attained. The wisest man in Greece knew that he knew nothing.[1]

To sum up, belief is the state in which what is present to the mind is not an objective reality, but a representation of this, namely a proposition, something that can be true or false. Knowledge is the state in which the objective reality itself is present to the mind. Knowledge therefore can be spoken of in the syntax of *connaître*, belief only in that of *savoir*; and conversely that which can only be spoken of in the syntax of *savoir* must remain on the level of belief. And it is when one sees that the mental content, at the level of belief, is a proposition or image of reality, that one can see how it can come about that beliefs can "roll about" on the scale which stretches from falsity to truth. So we need room for the conception that the mind forms images or reality (otherwise we cannot explain falsity), but we need also to retain the conception that the intellectual goal is to dispense with images and apprehend reality neat.

---

[1] We might compare this with two stages in knowing how to perform some activity, for example drive a car. There is the stage at which a man has to take each situation to bits, so to speak and represent it to himself piecemeal—"Turn right to avoid the bicycle, slow down because of the lorry." This man does not know how to drive, though he is learning. The man who knows how to drive simply responds to each total situation appropriately.

9

Dialectic and the Structure of Reality

THE discussion of falsity and negation in the *Sophist* is bound up with another theme which is of great importance to Plato in his later dialogues—the nature of dialectic or philosophical method. This can be divided into three topics, the *koinônia genôn* or "sharing of kinds", the importance of division, and the "letters and syllables" of reality.

The sharing of kinds

The young Socrates in the *Parmenides* seems to put forward two propositions:—(1) That a particular can partake in both of two incompatible general terms (both P and not-P can be predicable of S), and that it is somehow the relation of *participation* (the converse of *being predicable of*) which makes these antinomies possible; and (2) that antinomies only arise between general terms "in particulars" and not "among themselves" (incompatible predicates can cohabit the same particular but are not in any other way reconcilable). From this we can perhaps infer that he would also have assented to a third proposition: (3) that general terms are not predicable of each other. (For if they were, then one would partake in another, and, if it is participation that makes antinomies possible, it would be possible for antinomies to arise between general terms "among themselves"). S may be both P and Q (even where Q is incompatible with P); but P-hood can never be Q. A thing can be, for example, a table, but being a table cannot be, for example, being an artefact. Socrates must have gone away from Parmenides' demonstration, which shortly followed, convinced that Parmenides at any rate could make any antinomy appear at any level. Perhaps the imputation to the young Socrates of the view stated above, and the discomfiture which followed his profession of it, can be seen as a confession by Plato that he had wrongly taken something of the kind for granted himself. Certainly he lays great emphasis in his later writings on the doctrine that "kinds can share". Worrying perhaps over the view of those who said that "Jones is Jones" is true, and "Jones is bald" strictly false on the ground that Jones and the bald are not identical, he came to see (and to say in the *Sophist*) that there are essentially two kinds of statement: those which assert (or deny) identity, and those which attribute (or deny the attribution of) a predicate to a subject; and that this distinction applies at every level. He saw also that in an identity the left-hand side need not be verbally identical with the right-hand side. "Not-being is difference" is, he suggests, an example of a true identity-statement. The *Sophist* also goes at any rate some distance towards distinguishing these two uses of *to be* (its use in identities and in predications) from its use to assert existence. A formula at least is provided for each: *S partakes in P* for "P is predicable of S", *A partakes in sameness to B* for "A is identical with B", and *A partakes in the existent* for "A exists." And in a series of criticisms of various metaphysical doctrines Plato seems to wish to make the point that existence is a property of everything whatsoever, and cannot therefore be identified with any property (for example changelessness) which characterizes some things but not others.

The main emphasis, however, is upon the doctrine of the sharing of kinds, the doctrine that true predication-statements can be made at the level of general terms. We should want to ask whether the doctrine is extensional or intensional, whether it is about relations between classes or relations between properties. The phrase "sharing of kinds" suggests the former. The word *genos* which occurs in it means etymologically "race" and has come into English as "genus". This suggests (and a good deal supports the suggestion) that the kind of relationship Plato has in mind is that by which one race (say cats) forms part of a larger race (say animals). It seems to me, however, that Plato was not clear on this point. Certainly in the case of identity-statements Plato is not thinking of "race-relations" of this kind. That everything that has either of two properties also has the other is not enough to make two properties identical. That every P thing is a Q thing is enough to make the P partake in the Q; but it seems to me that Plato does not distinguish this situation from that in which "the P", or P-hood, is itself a Q-thing.[1] By using in his thought such phrases as "the P partakes in the Q" Plato seems to have failed to distinguish the case where "the P" denotes the class of P things, and the relationship to the Q is that of class-inclusion, from the case where "the P" denotes the class-property, and the relationship to the Q is that this second property characterizes the first. It was easy for him to confound the two since it is usually the case that, when the class of P things is included in the class of Q things, one can say that *being P* is a way of *being Q* (being a cat is a way of being an animal); a relationship between classes therefore seems to carry with it a relationship between properties, and *vice versa*. Sometimes, however, when one property "partakes in" another a corresponding relation between the classes does not obtain. Indefinability, for example might be definable without indefinables being a sub-class of definables. If I am right in thinking that Plato did not deem it important to distinguish relations between properties from relations between classes, it is interesting that this should be true of him, who had earlier laid so much stress on the importance of distinguishing "the beautiful itself" from the class of beautiful things. A notion that relations between classes are determined by relations between properties might have led him to think that the two would always go in parallel, so that (at the level of participation between general terms) S things would be P things if and only if the S, so to speak, permitted this by partaking in the P.[2]

---

[1] EPD 2, pp. 401–10.

[2] It must be remembered that Plato was not in possession of any satisfactory terminology for the discussion of such matters. He certainly had no words that meant "property" or "class", nor any idiom that unambiguously distinguished a particular property from the class corresponding to it. He could not therefore ask himself such a question as: "How are relations between classes related to relations between properties?". At best he could have availed himself of some such cumbrous formulation as: "When one race forms part of another race, then does that by which

Dialectic and the Structure of Reality

But the predominant strain in the notion of the sharing of kinds is, I think, the idea that general terms or "kinds" belong to a sort of hierarchy or family tree, in such a way that the typical general term will be a version of one above it, and will itself have its own versions below it, in the way in which *being a cat* is a way or version of *being an animal*, and has below it its own versions such as *being a Siamese cat*. This of course can only come about if there is present in, say, cats both the unifying factor, animality, which they share with dogs and cows, and also the diversifying factor or factors which distingusih them. And these factors must be capable of entering into these relationships without thereby destroying their self-identity. There could not be predatory animals if *animality* could not admit *predatoriness*, just as, perhaps, there cannot be dead souls because *being a soul* cannot admit *being dead*. A property such as animality is, so to speak, plastic in that it is capable of being realized in many specific ways, by accepting modification by other properties such as predatoriness; but it is not indefinitely plastic, it has a nature or self-identity of its own, out of which it cannot be moulded; and this determines what combinations of factors there can or cannot be.[1]

When Plato talks about the one and the many, or unity and multiplicity, in his later writings, he tends to have in mind the relationship between the unity of, let us say, a genus, and the multiplicity of its species. A "heavenly tradition" in the *Philebus* has taught us that discourse is possible because "things are made of one and many and have limit and limitlessness in them". This means, I think, that a "thing" or property is almost always a unity which comprehends many diversities (in the way in which animality comprehends cat-hood, dog-hood and so on), and that there is always a finite number of these diverse specific versions, though each of these can be realized in an infinite number of instances; and that the possibility of making true statements about general terms depends on this

[1] In my opinion Plato makes this point in the *Sophist*; EPD 2, pp. 411–16.

the one race is one form part of that by which the other race is one?". Or perhaps: "If the race of men is part of the race of animals, then will the man itself form part of the animal itself?". What he managed to achieve with such language is remarkable; equally however our interpretation of these achievements must be somewhat precarious.

fact. This passage also emphasizes how difficult it may be in certain cases to find the "one common nature" (*idea*) which is always present in every true kind, and also to divide the kind into its subkinds.

Collection and division

This leads on to the place of the two activities of "collection" and "division" in dialectic or philosophical method. By the word "collection" Plato sometimes seems to intend the sort of synoptic survey by which we grasp the range of some general term by bringing together the disparate things which it comprehends—as when a man sees that lunacy, love and poetic inspiration all have in common a feature which enables us to call them all forms of madness. Collection in this sense of the word is an activity which is presumably preliminary to that of seeking "the one common nature" whose presence in all the members of the collection genuinely unites them. Before we ask the Socratic question what madness essentially is, we must first "collect" it so that we see what it comprehends; then we must go on—and this may be difficult—to see what its disparate parts have in common that makes them all versions of madness. Collection, however, Plato repeatedly stresses, needs to be accompanied by division. The significance of this is clearly brought out in the *Philebus*. In this dialogue Socrates' opponent Protarchus argues that, since some pleasures are good, all must be; otherwise pleasures would not be a homogeneous class. Protarchus' fallacy is to assume that a class must be homogeneous in respects other than that whereby its members qualify for membership of it. In the *Phaedrus* Socrates is made to give a lengthy demonstration of the dangers of this assumption. He denounces love because it is a form of madness, his implicit train of thought being that, since lunacy is a form of madness and is bad, love, being also a form of madness, must be bad as well. His mistake, as he sees, was to fail to divide madness into the two kinds, divine and morbid, to locate love in the former and lunacy in the latter, and so to praise love while condemning lunacy. In the *Philebus* it is suggested that Protarchus' fallacy is bound up with failure to realize that "kinds can share". Those who suppose that all pleasures must be alike (all good, for example, or all bad) fail to see that the race of pleasures may be unified by one factor and diversified by many others. Pleasures, they think, are pleasures. They do not ask what it is that unifies the race of pleasures, and so they assume that each of its members is simply a pleasure and nothing else; it is easy to proceed from here to the conclusion that the members must all be alike. If they were different, they argue, they would not all be pleasures. Therefore from the intuitive act, by which we "collect" some class by observing the similarity between disparate pleasures, for example, or disparate kinds of madness, we have to proceed in two directions. We have to proceed "upwards" or "inwards" to an explicit grasp of what the factor is which is present in the whole range, and we have to proceed "downwards" or "outwards" to an explicit grasp of the other factors with which this factor may be combined, and thus to an explicit grasp of the segments into which the range is to be sub-divided. If for example we saw that in the case of madness the essence or unifying factor was something like inattention to ordinary mundane considerations, then we could go on to see that this could be brought about either by disease of the mind or by its concentration on higher things. This would give us the distinction between morbid and divine madness. We should no longer think that there was on the one hand madness, one monolithic thing, having multitudinous instances, all of these being instances of the same thing and therefore similar to each other. We should see that the monolith was not a monolith but on the contrary an essence realizable in different forms, and that the same no doubt was true of these; and that we do not get to the level at which we can say "and this has infinitely many instances, and there is no significant difference between them", until we have discovered all the various significantly different forms in which the essence can be realized, all the various diversifying factors which can be combined with the unifying factor to produce not just different things but different kinds of things.

Letters and syllables of reality

This is all so familiar to us that it risks being tedious. We are seldom tempted to think that a common characteristic can turn up in only one form, and that therefore all its instances must be alike in all important respects. But this is only because we have learnt the grammar of abstract thought. By an effort of the imagination we can see that it must have been an essential part of prising off the level of abstract discourse to see how, and through what degrees, a character like animality is related to its instances. It is part of what is involved in seing what a character is. A model which Plato used to bring out his meaning to those to whom it was less familiar was that of letters and syllables. We first encounter this in the *Cratylus*. In this dialogue Plato puts forward ideas about the nature of language. He sees that for a language to be useful the distinctions that it draws must exist in reality, and that if it is generally understood to what a word refers, then the phonetic characteristics of the word are unimportant. He also sees, however, that languages commonly work to some extent by building compound words out of simpler ones, as we form "lion-tamer" to denote one who tames lions; and he toys with the idea that perhaps languages ought to be formed entirely in this way. (It is suggested that such a language would be philosophically illuminating because the structure of the language would display the structure of reality. But, as Socrates retorts, such a language could only be constructed if the philosophical illumination was already available). If a language were to be constructed entirely in this way, reasonable economy would only be served if there existed in reality a fairly small number of essential characteristics (all other characteristics being combinations of these); then we could distinguish these elementary characteristics, and allot a sound to each of them. It is suggested that the principle of allotment might be affinity; the sound should imitate the essence of the characteristic. (If we suppose that *f* imitates water, *i* imitates animality and *sh* imitates gliding motion, then *fish* would be the proper name for swimming aquatic animals). In a language constructed on these principles we could tell from a glance at a word what were the essential characteristics of the realities which it named.

Plato may perhaps have thought that languages did to some extent grow up in this way, though he sees both that historical accidents have distorted the Greek language from being a language of this kind, and also that it is none the worse for that.

Dialectic and the Structure of Reality

But what is of interest, and what recurs in several other dialogues, is the notion that reality has a structure which could be "imitated" in language in this way. It can readily be seen that this is a model for the notion of collection and division, and for the metaphysical doctrine underlying this conception of philosophical method. The kind of general term which a philosopher is likely to try to understand better—statesmanship, for example—can be regarded as a syllable. That is to say, it is likely to be a specific form of something more generic; statesmanship is a specific form of knowledge. Trying to see what statesmanship is is trying to spell it out into its letters. The *Statesman* suggests that all the letters in every syllable are familiar to us; there are no difficult letters, only difficult combinations of letters. This is what makes analogies possible. Statesmanship for example is analogous to weaving; both involve knowing how to combine the tough and the pliable in such a way as to make the whole cohere. To say this is to say that statesmanship and weaving are similar syllables since many of the letters in each are the same.

It is suggested in the *Sophist* that some combinations of letters or essential characters are possible and some impossible; that there are certain factors which are, like vowels, responsible for the possibilities of combinations, and other factors which are responsible for the impossibilities; and that the true philosopher will know what is possible and what is not. If Plato supposed that there exists any *a priori* theory of what characters can and cannot be combined, he does not tell us what it is. Rather he seems to suggest, as we said earlier, that a factor can enter into all and only those combinations which do not impair its self-identity. In that case when we are trying to "spell" a complex character like statesmanship we have no theory to tell us how to proceed. Plato seems to suggest two techniques for spelling-out a syllable into its letters, one mechanical and one intuitive; and he seems also to suggest, whether deliberately or otherwise, that the mechanical technique is useless except under the guidance of insight. According to the mechanical technique we first subsume the syllable which we are trying to spell under a very general heading; statesmanship is a kind of knowledge. Next we divide knowledge into two, making sure, so far as we can, that the two divisions are so to speak of equal weight, and that each has some genuine common feature.[1] So we divide knowledge into theoretical knowledge and practical, discard the one of these under which statesmanship does not fall, and proceed to divide the one under which it does fall in the same way as before. We go on doing this until we arrive at statesmanship. Unfortunately, however, when Plato's Eleatic Stranger uses this technique to define sophistry (in the *Sophist*) and statesmanship (in the *Statesman*) it misfires and he defines the wrong thing; it only works properly on its first demonstration run where it is used to define an angler. This seems to suggest the very Platonic conclusion that there are no mechanical substitutes for thinking; and the man who has to try to spell out a difficult syllable must fall back on the other, the intuitive technique. This is, simply, to think of an analogy, of something that seems to one to have some affinity to the concept which is giving trouble, to define the analogous concept, and to see whether this gets one anywhere. It is, in this way, by analysing weaving that the Stranger eventually manages to analyse statesmanship. By an imaginative act, presumably, he divines a similarity of structure between weaving and statesmanship. The essentials of weaving are comparatively easy to diagnose; if the analogy between weaving and ruling holds, then the same essentials, or some of them, will be among the essentials of ruling; we try whether they are, and find that in fact they are—ruling also is an art of combination, and so on. In this way we discover what ruling essentially is.

It is difficult to know whether Plato thought (as the analogy of spelling might suggest) that a quality such as statesmanship consisted of a certain arrangement of certain essential elements, rather as a molecule consists of a certain arrangement of certain atoms, or whether he thought that the syllables of reality could be spelt in many equally correct ways. There are a good many obscurities in the doctrines to be found in the later dialogues about the manner in which "kinds can share"—about the relationships which obtain between general terms. There was a sequel projected to the *Sophist* and *Statesman*—the *Philosopher*—

---

[1] We divide into two wherever we can do so without infringing the other conditions; but it is allowed that this is not always possible and we may have to divide into three or more.

and it seems never to have been written. Perhaps the reason was that Plato failed to answer the questions that we want to ask about the meaning of the hints which are dropped in the dialogues he did write. But it is obvious that his mind was actively concerned with the relationships, such as that of genus and species, which can obtain between general terms, and that he thought that general terms can be arranged in some sort of hierarchical structure. Those at the top of the structure were more generic and pervasive than those lower down; those lower down were somehow combinations of those above. It seems probable that Plato made the mistake of putting at the very top of his hierarchy characters like existence and unity which characterize everything whatsoever, as if these were one degree more generic and pervasive than those like being an organism which characterize very many things but not all.

Perhaps the notion of the sharing of kinds can be seen more clearly if we look at it from the cosmological end. When the Craftsman, in Timaeus' myth, proceeds to the ordering of chaos, he resolves that this indeterminate sea should become definite; reason demands that it should become some one definite existent thing. To meet this demand it must be ordered and have some character; but it can be ordered in many ways and have many characters. Reason declares that the best character it can have is that of a living creature, and so it becomes corporeal (an organized enduring physical system) and also spiritual. To be a living creature, therefore, is one way, the best way, of realizing the extremely "open" property of being a single existing somewhat; and living creature-hood is made up of corporeality blent with spirituality. The living creature, therefore, is the existent somewhat blent with, or participating in, the corporeal and the spiritual. Reason also demands that the universe should be a living creature whose parts are themselves, so far as possible, living creatures; and that every subordinate version of living-creature-hood should be realized in it. So we get to celestial living creatures with bodies of fire, to terrestrial living creatures with composite bodies, and to whatever other general kinds there may be. The essence of a terrestrial living creature is presumably the open property of living-creature-hood realized in a certain material—living-creature-hood, perhaps, participating in a specific kind of corporeality. But the property of being a terrestrial living creature is still a very open property; you could not make anything which was just an instance of that. "Make a terrestrial living creature" is an instruction that one could not act upon without taking numerous decisions of a general kind; for example what manner of locomotion the creature is to have, how it is to nourish itself, how defend itself, and so on. To arrive at the sort of general term of which an apprentice,[1] so to speak, could be expected to make a specimen without referring to his master for further instructions, we have to blend living-creature-hood with a certain manner of locomotion, of nutrition and the rest. At some point we shall arrive at, say, the general design of the predatory mammal (or the vegetarian insect, and so on). The predatory mammal will be the essence of the terrestrial living creature participating in a certain kind of locomotion, a certain kind of nutrition, a certain choice from each of the other possibilities which the essence of the terrestrial living creature leaves open. But the predatory mammal is itself a possibility which can be actualized in various ways by taking various decisions of principle about the sort of living creature that is required. It is only when we have taken these decisions and arrived at, say, the essence of the lion or the wolf, by blending the essence of the predatory mammal with a selection from each of the possibilities still left open, that we have at last something that could be handed over to the apprentice with the instruction that he should work out the technical details of epidermis, nervous system, digestive organs and so on. The lion, therefore, as an essence will be the predatory mammal blended with each of the decisions of principle which we made in arriving at the instructions for the apprentice; it will partake in predatory-mammal-hood (and therefore in whatever that partakes in right up to unity and existence), and also in largeness and all the other things which define what kind of predatory mammal the lion is to be. And actual lions will be this design realized in appropriate material.

This may give some idea of the way in which a "syllable" or specific nature like the lion could be constituted by "letters" or more generic natures; and correspondingly of how kinds can

---

[1] The apprentice is an expository device of my own; he does not represent anything in the *Timaeus*.

share. I have, deliberately but perhaps unjustly, used notions belonging to the *sharing*-family in different ways. I have made the lion partake in what is "above" it (the predatory mammal, the large and so on), and I have also made the predatory mammal partake in, or be blended with, the factors such as largeness which are "on the same level" as it is in the sense that they co-operate with it in generating the lion. I have done this because I suspect, though without much definite reason, that Plato was more enthusiastic about the doctrine that kinds can share than clear about exactly what he meant by it. If, however, this account does any justice to Plato's rather inchoate ideas (as I believe they were) about the relationship between more generic and more specific characters, it must remain an open question whether he would have wanted seriously to say that syllables such as sophistry and statesmanship, which are not the essences of natural kinds, can be regarded as made up of letters in a manner analogous to syllables like the lion, which are the essences of natural kinds. And if he would have wanted to say that the kind of syllables in which he was most interested (those like sophistry and statesmanship) were analogous to those which are essences of natural kinds, it must remain an open question how the analogy was to be worked out.

10

The Good Life

WE now have some idea of the world in which man finds himself. It is a physical world, and therefore to some extent an alien world (for man as a thinking, hoping, fearing, loving, hating thing is not a physical being); and it is a world which is always liable to lapse back into the natural condition of the physical, namely chaos and indeterminacy. But it is also an ordered world containing determinate things, and it has this character because reason is efficacious in it. The essential interests of reason, however, have nothing to do with the physical realm; a whole series of steps has to be traversed before we can get from the abstract principles of rational order to the organization of the world which embodies or reflects these principles. For this reason it is a puzzling world; for that which solves problems is reason and the demands of reason are connected only by this series of steps to the problems which call for our attention.

Man who inhabits this world is a subordinate source of order within it. His business is to render orderly and intelligible his own behaviour, and as much of the environment as he can control. But he has in himself a principle of disorder, because, although he is essentially a rational being, it was necessary for him, if he was to be a subordinate source of order in the cosmos, to be given a body wherewith to act upon his environment, and to become sensitive to the needs and disorders of that body in the form of desires and feelings, which make clamant demands upon him, but which are liable to be inconsistent both with his felicity and with his business of ordering his corner of the world.

Furthermore the principles upon which he is to proceed are all to be recovered from within himself (for he is an intelligence, not just a slave of intelligence; to that extent he is autonomous, and the demands that he has to comply with are his own demands); but the work of regaining an explicit grasp of these principles is of the utmost difficulty, because, although he could not think at all unless he used these principles in his thought, nevertheless he uses them inevitably in a concrete form which is, as we have seen, far removed from their origin in the principles of rational order as such.

So much by way of background to Plato's discussions of the problems of human life. Most of the dialogues which concern themselves with what we should call topics of moral philosophy belong to the earlier part of Plato's life and terminate in the *Republic*, which may well be looked on as his summing-up of his contribution to ethics. After the *Republic*, apart from the *Philebus*, his remarks about problems of morals tend to be perfunctory. This does not apply so strongly to problems of political and social life, and it would be a serious misrepresentation of Plato's thought to suppose that he would have made any wide separation between moral and political problems. It would, however, be partly correct to say that Plato moved, some time about the middle of his working life, from a predominant concern with ethics to a predominant concern with logic, metaphysics and theory of knowledge.

The early dialogues commonly present Socrates asking the question what is friendship, courage, temperance or some similar quality or relation. He tends to address his question to somebody who seems to possess the quality in question, and therefore ought to know what it is. The answer he gets is usually halting and easily shown to be inadequate; and at this state some bystander sometimes intervenes with a confident formula derived from some philosopher—sometimes Socrates himself—and has to be shown that he cannot defend it and has not understood it. The dialogues then commonly end in perplexity with Socrates sadly observing that they none of them know what so-and-so is. These inquiries can be regarded as searches for definitions, so long as it is remembered that the definitions sought for are Socratic definitions. There is no question of trying to settle the meaning of a word. Everybody is agreed,

The Good Life

more or less, in the *Charmides*, what temperance is, or, in the *Laches*, what courage is, in the sense that everybody is agreed, more or less, what conduct does and what does not count as a manifestation of these qualities. True they are inclined to offer an account of the quality in question from which it would follow that some action ordinarily thought to display it would not in fact do so; but when this consequence is drawn by Socrates, the account tends to be retracted. It is true that in the *Euthyphro* there is some disagreement about what sort of conduct counts as piety (about whether it is pious to prosecute your father for murder), though here too the meaning of the word is generally agreed, in that everybody knows that piety has something to do with the demands of religion. But apart from the *Euthyphro* (and even that is only a partial exception) these discussions tend to take as a datum something like this: that to do *a*, *b* and *c* would be to display the quality in question, and to do *d*, *e* and *f* would be to fail to display it; and the purpose of the discussion is to find some theoretical account of why this virtuous quality requires one to do *a*, *b* and *c* and to abstain from *d*, *e* and *f*. Doubtless it is the normal assumption that although *a*, . . . *f* are all clear cases, and their relationship to the quality in question can be taken as a starting-point from which to investigate it, nevertheless there will be other cases such as *j*, *k*, *l* whose relationship to the quality in question is obscure; and part of the purpose of the discussion is to try to understand how to determine these problematical cases. (Thus if we can decide what piety really is we shall be able to decide whether it is more impious to prosecute one's father for murder or to allow a murder to go unexpiated). The setting of the *Laches* makes what is in this context an interesting sociological point. It is that the increasing complexity of modern life is what has made these problems urgent. In the earlier part of the fifth century the ethos of the city had been a sufficient educational influence and children had been given no formal moral guidance by their parents; now in a more complex and intellectually varied world questions of principle have to be settled by parents if their children are to be rightly instructed.

It would be foolish to suggest that Plato must have held consciously from the very beginning the conception of philosophical method which he was eventually to come to. But we can still ask whether we get a clearer understanding of his earlier writings if we suppose their composition to have been guided by something like this conception. With regard to the present topic, it seems that we do. Socratic definition is rather a puzzling process. "What", we want to ask, "is Socrates trying to do when he asks what, say, justice is? He knows, more or less, what he thinks just and what unjust; and since he takes his opinions on these matters as data he can hardly propose to revise them. What, therefore, does he expect to find out if he gets a satisfactory answer to his question? And why does he think, as he does, that until this question has been answered he is in no position to ask further questions about justice, such as whether it is a good thing, and whether it benefits the just man?"

The answer that we shall give to these questions in the light of our general understanding of Plato's conception of philosophy is along the following lines. The application of moral distinctions is an important part of intellectual activity. It is because we are intelligent beings that we have the habit of dividing the courageous from the cowardly, the temperate from the intemperate, the just from the unjust. There must, therefore, be some real and intelligible difference, some *rationale*, some principle underlying each of these distinctions. Or at least it is a reasonable presumption that that is so, though it must remain a possibility in each case that the habit of distinguishing rests merely on the traditions of men, and involves no principle that is of interest to reason. But assuming that in the case of justice, for example, we are dealing with a distinction which exists not just "by custom" but "by nature", we still do not know at all what the principle may be by virtue of which the disparate things we call just are on one side of the divide, and those we call unjust on the other. We tell the sheep from the goats, but we cannot say how they really differ. Being unable to say how they really differ, we can go only by their evident features which we have learnt to recognize ("the many justs"); and this leaves us unable to extend the distinction from the cases with which experience has familiarized us to those that are novel. There are, therefore, two things that we cannot do, and that an understanding of the nature of justice would enable us to do; one is to take decisions of principle as to what justice requires in cases which traditional wisdom has not equipped us to deal with, the other is to determine whether or not the whole distinction between the just and the unjust, and the preference for the former over the latter, is truly a distinction which we make as rational beings, or rests merely on convention.

It could be objected to this line of interpretation that it fails to do justice to the savagery of Plato's comments on ordinary moral thought. This is comparable, he tells us in *Republic* 7, to people looking at the shadows of puppets cast on the wall of a cave by the light of a fire, and imagining that these are ultimate reality. If this is what Plato thinks of your and my ability to comment on human affairs, surely he is hardly likely to tell us that our comments must reflect intelligible distinctions grounded in the nature of reason. Thought-habits which he describes as slime can surely hardly be the data from which the philosopher can start. The answer to this objection must be, I think, that justice must be done both to Plato's view that whatever we do in thought is done because we are rational beings, and also to his view that whatever we do in thought is distorted by our "reliance on the senses", or by our concentration on those aspects of things which attract our attention in the light of our mundane and mercenary interests. The parable of the men imprisoned in the cavern itself seems to allow that there are two grades of thought which exist at the pre-philosophical level of common sense. Some men can be forced to rely on "reckoning and measurement" rather than appearances, and these men pass from believing in the shadows to believing in the superior reality of the puppets. These are the men who attain to the status of craftsmen in the practical arts, and to an analogous status in the affairs of daily life. Plato allows, in fact, that it is in principle possible that any idea that anybody has may be a case of accepting as real what is no more than a shadow of a puppet; and he holds that many ideas cherished by many people have in fact this status. But at the same time he thinks that the concepts employed even by the vulgarest of the vulgar are images of realities (so that if men have monstrous ideas about the nature of justice, that in itself shows that there must be such a thing as justice); and he thinks also that some men, by some divine dispensation, use these concepts well, in the sense that they can tell, in practice, instances of justice from instances of injustice. If you asked him how Socrates could tell that he and his friends were among those whose moral discriminations were sound enough to be used as starting-points in the search for the *rationale* of these discriminations, I suppose he would have had to reply that they could not tell this for certain, but that any man who sincerely desires a better understanding of morality will have to begin by putting his faith in those moral judgments of which he is entirely convinced; and if, in the process of discussion, his faith in some of them is shaken, at least he will have to retain his faith in the process of rational discussion which shakes them and re-makes them. It is probably fair to say that there is in all this a greater confidence in the power of tradition and good upbringing, and in the sanity of ordinary thought, than Plato ever admits to when he is commenting on the value of these things. Plato wanted to insist on the absolute liberty of philosophical thought, on the philosopher's unqualified right to challenge, in the name of reason, any belief, no matter how universal the assent to it. To this end he insists on the worthlessness of conventional opinion, and tends to forget that if no reliance whatever could be placed on anything which anybody thought at the pre-philosophical level, then the Socratic method could never get under way; for this method must presuppose that even you and I do sometimes know that this or that would be an instance of courage, say, or justice. Aristotle often says things like: "There must be some truth in anything that all decent men are agreed upon"; Plato would have found it difficult to say anything so complacent, so establishmentarian, so cramping to the radical liberty of critical thought. But one has to admit that Plato took for granted something not altogether unlike what his pupil openly said.

So when Socrates asks: "What is temperance?" we are to regard him as seeking insight into the intelligible principle which underlies our habit of dividing the temperate from the intemperate and treating the former as manifestations of a virtue or excellence, something which is "good" or in other words valuable, useful and worth preserving. If that is what Socrates is doing in these discussions, let us attend to some of the features of the way in which he does it. There are three things which are commonly to be found in a dialogue of this kind which are worth noticing.

1. When asked "What is V?" (where V is some virtue),

Socrates' friend tends to reply either by giving instances of V-like behaviour, or by naming some dispositions or character-traits in which, he thinks, V consists. Courage is holding one's ground in battle; temperance is being unobtrusive, being inclined to blush, and so on. Such answers Socrates tends to reject both on the general ground that he wants some single principle which unites the various manifestations, and also on the more particular ground that V cannot be simply a propensity to do certain things into the description of which "V" does not enter; at the least it must be a propensity to do these things in the right way, on the right occasions, and so on. There is a difference in fact between a virtue and a temperamental factor such as modesty in that a virtue only shows itself when it is called for, whereas a temperamental factor is a propensity to act in a certain way both when such actions is called for and when it is not. Animals can display the temperamental factor of boldness, or insensitivity to danger, but they cannot display the virtue of courage because they cannot distinguish the occasions when danger ought to be avoided from those when it ought to be faced.

2. A virtue, therefore, is a good thing. But this is puzzling because it must mean that it contributes something to the common good. If, however, one breaks the common good down into its components, it would seem that each of these components is the product of some special skill. If national defence is part of the common good, it is military skill that produces this, as it is medical skill that heals the sick, building skill which provides shelter, agricultural skill which gives us food, and so on. What, then, is the contribution to the common good which is made by temperance, justice or some other virtue? The question, of course, that this is designed to raise is the question why we attach value to the virtues. Are they things whose cultivation is important, or is the belief that this is so merely the survival of some primitive reverence?

3. An abstract noun such as "temperance", or a phrase such as "the just" can stand for the characteristic common to certain kinds of action (temperate action or just action), or it may stand for the characteristics common to certain kinds of men. The two cannot of course be divorced, but some confusion can be generated if they are not kept distinct. This becomes the more

The Good Life

important when the question that is being asked is: "What underlies the practice of separating the temperate from the intemperate?". For we shall now have to ask ourselves at some stage whether the important difference implicitly recognized by this practice is one between different spiritual constitutions or between different actions. Is it important that men should be of certain kinds (and incidentally act in certain ways), or that they should act in certain ways (and incidentally be of certain kinds)? There tends to be some confusion on this point in the earlier dialogues (in the *Euthyphro* "the pious" or "the holy" sometimes means piety as a quality of certain men, sometimes piety as a quality of certain actions, sometimes the practice of religion); and it would be difficult to hold that Plato was clear about the distinction. However there is a pattern to which these dialogues tend to conform. If Socrates succeeds in persuading his friend to treat the question "What is V?" as a request, not for instances of V, but for the principle which unites them, his friend tends to try to say what is the characteristic common to V-like actions, and Socrates himself tends to bring the discussion round to the question what is the characteristic common to V-like men.

These observations can be tied together by considering them in the light of the well-known paradoxes that Socrates is alleged to have propounded: that virtue is one; that virtue is knowledge; and that no man deliberately does something wrong. What underlies these paradoxes is a train of thought along the following lines. If we are right to value virtue, it must be something that does good. If it is something that does good, it must contribute to an end that we all want to achieve. But if, as is certainly the case, some men fail to cultivate virtue, we shall have to confess that these men are failing to cultivate the indispensable means to an end that they want to achieve. The only credible explanation of this is that they have misguided ideas about how to achieve it. Therefore the difference between good men and bad men must surely be an intellectual difference; the former know how to encompass the ends that we all want to encompass; the latter do not know, and therefore blunder, well-meaningly in one sense, but nevertheless disastrously. Several times in these early dialogues the discussion verges towards the admission that virtue is knowledge, or that some virtue is some kind of knowledge; but Socrates will never allow the admission to be made. If one of his friends, like Nicias in the *Laches* or Critias in the *Charmides*, says something which rests on the formula "Virtue is knowledge", he receives unsympathetic treatment. The midwife will not allow that a man who utters a formula which he cannot understand is giving birth to a child which deserves to live. However many may be the considerations that suggest that moral goodness is some kind of intellectual insight which enables a man to deploy his gifts and endowments in the right way, still it must be admitted that this notion has formidable difficulties. If the difference between bad men and good men is that the latter know how to live, then, since this knowledge can hardly be fragmented, moral goodness cannot be fragmented either; yet everybody knows that some men are brave and gluttonous, others temperate and cowardly. Again everybody knows that we all sometimes do, deliberately, what we know to be wrong, as if virtue were not something whose value we must all concede, but something which we are prepared to throw aside when pleasure beckons. Again if virtue were knowledge, then it ought to be possible to teach it; but everybody knows that it cannot be taught, either by parents, or by the Sophists, those itinerant public lecturers who undertook to teach their audiences any desirable accomplishment, including that of being a good citizen. Grant, then, that it may sometimes seem as if courage, for example, is the knowledge of what is and is not fearful. In other words, it may sometimes seem as if the brave are those who know what things do and do not hurt us, and who shun things like dishonour, which they know do us real harm, preferring to face things like pain and death which they know to be the preferable alternative in situations where the choice has to be made. But however strongly argument may incline us to sympathize with such a line of thought, we cannot accept it as satsifactory unless we can see how, in that case, courage can be seen to be something narrower than the knowledge of good and evil, something which is not the whole of moral goodness, but only a part.

So Socrates argues in the *Laches*. We know he does not really mean it; we know he thinks that courage is not an independent part of moral goodness, but merely one aspect of it, the aspect under which the knowledge of good and evil shows itself in the face of danger. But he will not, here or elsewhere, allow us to say this until we can also deal with the difficulties to which it gives rise. The *Euthydemus* advances arguments to show that that which differentiates good men from bad must be some kind of knowledge; for virtue can never be harmful, yet everything that can be of value can also be harmful unless we know how to use it rightly; but having got to this point Socrates shies away by raising and failing to answer the question what kind of knowledge this could be. The *Meno* employs roughly the same argument, and its treatment of it is worth some attention.

The question Meno wants to ask is: whether virtue can be taught. The question Socrates wants to settle first is the, to him, prior question what virtue is. Eventually he consents to consider Meno's question provided it is tied up with a provisional answer to his own. He seems to concede that we can sometimes only make philosophical progress by allowing ourselves to consider a subsequent question before we have settled a prior one, and that we may do this so long as we keep the relation between the two in mind. He allows, then, that if moral goodness is intellectual insight, it is likely that it is teachable; and he proceeds to show that it is not teachable by the argument that neither parents nor Sophists succeed in teaching it. Having, however, allowed that the proposition that virtue is, invariably, a good thing suggests that it is intimately bound up with knowledge, he does not, this time, allow the idea to drop altogether; he suggests that perhaps virtue is not knowledge but right belief. For if it is a matter, not of intellectual insight into how to live, but merely of having the right ideas on this subject, then it is intelligible both how it is that virtue is always a good thing (for that the virtuous man's opinions are correct will see to that) and also how it is that it cannot always be taught (for there is no reliable way of communicating correct ideas). It is difficult, and unnecessary, to believe that Plato thought this a satisfactory account of the nature of virtue. It is difficult to think so because it is difficult to doubt that he would have argued that no set of correct beliefs without insight would enable a man to deal with any but standard situations; it is unnecessary to think so because it is already plain (and the *Meno* makes it even plainer) that what is given by the ordinary parent and the ordinary Sophist is not teaching in Socrates' understanding of this process. For teaching, in Socrates' view, is midwifery; it consists in eliciting from the pupil what he already has in him. Therefore from the fact that admonition cannot give a young man insight into life, we cannot infer that such insight would not be elicited by a proper process of philosophical dialogue. The real conclusion, therefore, of the *Meno*, as opposed to the "dramatic" conclusion which ends the conversation, is twofold: firstly that if the factor which differentiates good men from bad men is an intellectual factor, then it is something like insight rather than assent to the correct propositions; secondly that it is possible to think of two levels of moral goodness, the one that of the man of insight (and this goodness will be always beneficial), the other that of the man in the street, resting on assent to the right propositions, and therefore not invariably to be relied upon to make the best contribution to every situation.

The *Republic* provides an answer to most of the questions raised in the earlier dialogues. It begins with a conversation between Socrates and Cephalus, an old man of the highest character—the sort of man whose moral judgments deserve respect. After some discussion of the question whether old age is burdensome, whether wealth is to be prized, and similar matters, Socrates asks Cephalus to say whether justice can be identified with telling the truth and paying one's debts, or whether such actions are sometimes just and sometimes unjust. Cephalus excuses himself—he is not going to meet Socrates on this level—and his son Polemarchus takes over. Polemarchus tries to say what he thinks is common to all just conduct—it consists in giving to each what is fitting. He cannot, however, defend himself against Socrates, he cannot say how the just man knows in each case what the fitting thing is, and he cannot find a contribution of any significance which justice makes to common welfare. He commits himself to the view that to give to each what is fitting means that one should do good to one's friends and harm to one's enemies, but he is easily persuaded to substitute for this the formulation that one should do good to good men and harm to evil ones. While Socrates is trying to persuade him that nothing which is essentially good can consist in part in doing harm to anything, the conversation is interrupted by the Sophist Thrasymachus who maintains energetically that it is obvious to any emancipated man that "just conduct" is simply the conduct which is convenient to the establishment in any society, and which they therefore enjoin; from which he draws the conclusion that no man of any common sense and independence of mind will trouble to conform to the rules of just conduct except in so far as non-conformity is dangerous.

This introduction to Plato's most elaborate discussion of moral problems sets the stage for the discussion very subtly. Cephalus represents the matured wisdom of the men of an earlier generation. He is a man of probity who can be relied on to act and judge rightly, but he sees no need to seek the foundations of right conduct. His son Polemarchus has been influenced by the intellectual questioning of his generation, but he is a man of no intellectual vigour, and he is content with a formula which he has taken from a poet of acknowledged wisdom. He shows some sympathy with an earlier world of tribal loyalites when he says that the just man is useful to his friends and baneful to his enemies, but he is civilized enough to see that this will not do. So far traditional ideas of right and wrong have been defended by two men of admirable character and comfortable circumstances, the first of whom will not and the second of whom cannot provide any rational basis for these ideas. The effect of this is shown by the interruption of Thrasymachus. In default of any rational justification of moral rules it is inevitable that men of active mind will assert that they are products of human convention and deserve no respect from anybody capable of an open-eyed pursuit of his own well-being.

The *Republic*, therefore, is to defend, if not the traditional views of right and wrong, at least the traditional practice of distinguishing right from wrong, against the challenge of those who say that this practice is in origin nothing more than part of the propaganda-machinery deployed by the governing classes. The question which it chooses to consider for this purpose is the question "What is justice?". This question could be interpreted as the question "What is a just act?" or as the question "What is a just man?". Socrates' companions take it, to begin with, in the first sense, Socrates himself in the second. His purpose, therefore, is to try to understand what is the state of character by virtue of which some men are able always to act rightly towards their neighbours; and he hopes also, of course, to find that the answer to this question will be such as to confute Thrasymachus' view that no man who is clear-sightedly concerned with his own well-being will try to be just.

When he arrives at the answer to his question he makes plain what is the relation between just actions and just men. To understand the nature of justice, and to see it to be a good thing, is to understand a certain state of character; and just actions, just institutions and so on are those which preserve, or proceed from, this state of character. To generalize this, we can say that in Plato's view the primary application of a word of moral praise is to a certain spiritual state, its application elsewhere being logically subordinate to this. Just as health is primarily a state of body, and the test whether we can call healthy a food or a seaside resort is whether it ministers to health, so goodness is primarily a state of the person and the test whether we can call conduct good is whether such conduct ministers to goodness. What matters in the end is that there should be certain sorts of men, not that certain sorts of action should be done; actions are to be judged in the light of the character they build, or issue from, not the other way round.

Justice in society is that by virtue of which the society is orderly, efficient and at peace with itself; injustice is that which creates strife, division, waste and misery. The essence of the moral teaching of the *Republic* is that the factor which creates injustice in society is the intelligible but misguided pursuit by most men of ends the achievement of which cannot give true satisfaction. Traditional moral teaching and the traditional notion of just conduct are designed to hold in check the pursuit of these ends and thus to restrain that which sets men in conflict with each other. This is the reason why we all think that the rules of just conduct ought to be upheld by others; for we should all like other people to be prevented from causing inconvenience. And that the ends whose pursuit creates injustice are not in reality worth pursuing is a clinching reason why we should impose the rules of just conduct upon ourselves. We do not sacrifice our well-being by accepting these restraints; that we do so is the great error which seduces men into behaving as immorally as their fears of punishment, human or divine, allow them to. The ignorance which makes men wicked is the ignorant belief that the only case for virtue is that vengeance awaits the wicked; for the shrewd can see that this case is hollow.

What then is the case for virtue? It can be stated on two levels. On the more exalted level we can say that virtue (or justice or whatever name you prefer to call it by) is that which is in accordance with man's rational nature and has the beauty and orderliness and efficiency which appeal to this nature. On the less exalted level the case for virtue is that, so far from involving a sacrifice of one's own well-being, it involves an enormous increment of it; for the temptations which prompt us to injustice are not in fact worth yielding to. Pleasure, or happiness, is not the same thing as the gratification of desire. When Sophocles in his old age lost his sexual virility he lost some of his desires and with them the possibility of their gratification; but he gained in contentment, so he said, by the transaction.[1]

Why is it that the temptations which prompt us to injustice are not worth yielding to? The answer is in terms of a human personality or soul. There are, as we saw earlier, three elements in each man. There is first the rationality which is his essential characteristic. This has twin fruits. It is because he is a rational being that a man desires to understand, and enjoys understanding, appreciates order and harmony, loves beauty, and desires to reproduce these where he can; and it is also in virtue of his rationality that a man is capable of prudent action, of consulting his long-term welfare and of organizing his conduct so as to achieve it. (Since prudence is the imposition of order upon one's own life, these two fruits are really one). The next element in every man is the element of spirit or self-respect, the element by virtue of which a man will not allow himself to be pushed around either by his own passions or by other men, the element by virtue of which we tend to behave so as to command the respect of others, the element which makes us lovers of honour and renown. The last element is the appetitive or acquisitive, the element by virtue of which we are susceptible to organic desires and gratifications and behave so as to guarantee ourselves the means for these gratifications.

The intention of the scheme of things is that a man should identify himself with his rationality—should be, what he really

[1] *Republic* Book I.

is, a lover of rational order—and that he should indulge his other propensities only in so far as their promptings assist him to discharge his responsibilities as an incarnate source of order; he should gratify his desire to eat only in so far as this desire is a signal of the body's needs. A man who lives in this way will be enormously much happier than a man who lives in any other way; for the pleasures of the mind are greater than the pleasures of the body, and the orderly gratification of the promptings of spirit and appetite under the guidance of prudence offers us everything that can be got from their disordered gratification, with the added advantage that stress and conflict are eliminated.[1] Moreover, a man who lives in this way will do no harm to anybody; he will be a spring of justice, not of injustice, a source of social well-being. For the order, harmony, efficiency, truth and beauty that he pursues are the only things which can, in the end, offer true happiness to anyone. It is in so far as a man attaches undue importance to the promptings of spirit and appetite (pursues too vigorously renown, or carnal satisfactions and the wealth that buys them) that he becomes a source of conflict. The just man, therefore, the man who can be relied upon always to "give to each what is fitting" and to sustain the common well-being, this man is the man who subordinates his spirited and appetitive propensities to his rationality; and he is also the man who lives happily. The source of moral and social ugliness is the misguided belief that happiness is to be found in the pursuit of glory or the gratification of desire, and in the misguided readiness to pursue it there.

This is the ethical theory of the *Republic*, and also, as far as I can see, the ethical theory that Plato subscribed to throughout his life. It answers the questions of the earlier dialogues about the relation between goodness and insight in something like the following way. Virtue is the kind of conduct which we are obliged to approve of and enjoin, the kind of conduct, that is to say, which in others, makes them useful and not harmful to us, and which, in ourselves, makes us tolerable to ourselves; and the knowledge which makes a man love virtue is the knowledge that a human being is, in the end, a rational soul, and that happiness is not to be identified with the gratification of

---

[1] It is a mistake to think that Plato was a puritan. The *Laws* opens with a defence of occasional intoxication, and the *Symposium* depicts a very gay party.

impulse but with the rational organization of the whole of life, and with the pursuit, so far as each man is capable of it, of the proper interests of the mind. To this we may add, perhaps, the knowledge of the ways in which various combinations of character and circumstance affect the personality—information which we need for the conduct of life.

The man who possesses this understanding of life will surely manifest moral goodness in all its forms. He will do so, at any rate, if his rational and spirited propensities have received the kind of early training which is able to bring out their potentialities. The *Republic*, therefore, defines the various moral virtues all in terms of the good functioning and right relationship of the "parts of the soul". What are we to say then of the man who is brave but gluttonous, or the man who is temperate but proud, or the man whose moral principles desert him in temptation? The *Republic* accommodates these men by distinguishing two levels of moral goodness, that which depends on insight and is therefore unitary, and that which depends on right belief, and is therefore presumably fragmentable. It holds that the first kind of virtue demands considerable intellectual powers. It seems to believe, rather confusedly, that only a man who is capable of insight into all the problems of philosophy can understand that which a man has to understand in order to know how to live. (This confusion is perhaps partly due to the fact that Plato tries to consider the question of the nature of moral goodness simultaneously with the question who is capable of ruling, i.e. of taking decisions of principle). Holding this view Plato seems to argue that for the generality of men the understanding of the nature of life that they are capable of can consist only of subscription to true propositions which a good upbringing has commended to them. (In the imaginary city which Socrates creates in the *Republic* such men—i.e. nearly all of us—are subjected to propaganda, surrounded by cultural influences designed to build up the conscience through the imagination, and subordinated to the rule of the philosophers). It is an odd paradox that although Plato thought it worthwhile writing his dialogues, and presumably hoped that some people would understand them, all the same, in the *Republic* at any rate, he refuses to place confidence in any philosophical understanding that falls short of total insight, something which he confesses to be far beyond the reach of Socrates, or in other words of himself; and he seems to think that those who do not understand absolutely do not understand at all, and cannot, if they get things right, owe this to anything but the good fortune which has conditioned them into the right opinion.

Virtue and the Pursuit of Happiness

THE man whose moral principles desert him in the face of temptation is of course the man whose morality is on the level of belief rather than insight. The *Meno* has suggested that it is characteristic of right belief that it is unstable; and the propaganda and the ceaseless censorship of cultural media which Socrates provides in his Republic are designed to counter this instability.

Nobody, therefore, does what he knows to be wrong (and in this sense nobody deliberately does what is wrong) because those who do wrong things do not *know* anything about right and wrong. Indeed when Plato considers this matter in the *Protagoras* he seems to argue that nobody even does what he *believes* to be wrong, if "believes" is taken in an occurrent rather than a dispositional sense. The account which Plato gives of *akrasia* (of doing something contrary to one's principles under temptation) is that what happens in such a case is that a man does an action which he ordinarily believes and says to be wrong but which momentarily, under the influence of temptation, he almost believes to be right.

The *Protagoras* gives a rather striking explanation of how this can happen to a man whose moral principles are on the level of belief. It argues that the man in the street identifies the good and the pleasant, in the sense that he judges to be good any course of conduct which leads to a balance of pleasure or happiness in the long run. It bases this on the assumption that it is impossible for a man to take what seems to him the less attractive course. But it holds that while this is in fact the way in which the man in the street forms his moral judgments, nevertheless he does not consciously admit this. We do not consciously allow the equation of the good to the pleasant. (Socrates is shocked that one who makes such pretensions to clear thinking as Protagoras should also refuse to allow this equation). We imagine that "wrong" means something other than "unpleasant on balance". For this reason we do not see that it is important to devise an "art of measurement" by which we can arrange things on a scale of pleasantness. If we had such a scale we should know which games are, and which are not, worth the candle; and such knowledge, it is suggested, could not be shaken by temptation. If I know that the party is never worth the hang-over, the attractiveness of heavy drinking could not persuade me to indulge in it; knowing it to be the less attractive course, I should be unable to take it. If, therefore, my condemnation of drunkenness was consciously, what it is unconsciously, namely a recognition that it is never worth it, then my condemnation of drunkenness would not "run away" under temptation. Since, however, I merely tell myself that drunkenness is "wrong" (not knowing what I mean by this), in this case as the party approaches I can easily tell myself that the game is after all worth the candle, because it is easy to distort the relative pleasurability of something which is near in time and something that is remote. I can therefore go to a party intending to get drunk, something which I condemn at other times as shameful behaviour. Perhaps I can even confess at the time that it is shameful behaviour, but in one sense I cannot really *believe* that it is; for to believe that it is shameful behaviour would be (for me, at any rate, as a man in the street) to be aware, perhaps unconsciously, that it is behaviour that does not pay; and such awareness would make it impossible for me to embark upon the course. My normal estimate of the relative pleasurability of the factors involved is disturbed by the proximity of the temptation, and that is how I yield.

We are forced to ask what explanation Plato would have offered for his belief that a man who really knows what moral goodness is can be relied upon always to act rightly. Three explanations seem available. One is to rule that by definition "know" is to entail "act accordingly". Such a ruling, however, is pointless in default of some reason for thus linking these *prima facie* distinct concepts; and this explanation, while its availability as a further shot always in the locker may have helped Plato to find the others plausible, cannot have done the work on its own. The second explanation is that the process of coming to understand what moral goodness is, being the restoration of the soul to its true nature as a lover of order, carries with it a detestation of whatever is disorderly and therefore of whatever is base. The third explanation is that which is suggested by the passage in the *Protagoras* which we have just considered, namely that the excellence of the good life consists in its being the happy life, and that therefore (since each man inevitably pursues his own happiness) we cannot know what the good life is without being inflexibly disposed to pursue it.

This raises the question of Plato's attitude to hedonism, or the doctrine that nothing can count as goodness unless the pursuit of it increases the happiness of the pursuer. This is a difficult topic, and one which excites passions among students of Plato. An essential preliminary to the discussion of it is to distinguish "vulgar hedonism" from "philosophical hedonism". Vulgar hedonism is the recommendation to pursue as many as possible of the activities vulgarly thought to be pleasurable—wine, women and song for short. Philosophical hedonism is the view that nothing can be good unless it is pleasant on balance, without any preconceptions as to what satisfies this condition. Plato's hostility to vulgar hedonism is of course implacable throughout; it was the inordinate pursuit of wine, women and song which made the pursuer into a social menace, and his own worst enemy. But that is not to say that he never felt tempted to trump the vulgar hedonist by offering to fight him on his own ground. "Very well", one says, "let us allow that a man cannot be asked to sacrifice his own happiness, or pleasure, and indeed could not respond if he were asked to do so. But do you not see that the pursuit of 'the pleasures' is the way to miss pleasure? The pleasure of 'the pleasures' is very much inferior to the pleasure of sobriety, and the inordinate pursuit of them generates stresses, within oneself, and between a man and his fellows, which ruin happiness."

There is not the slightest doubt that Plato did sometimes argue in this way. In order, perhaps, to explain why people mistakenly identify pleasure or well-being with the gratification of desire, and therefore devote themselves to "the pleasures", he has an argument which he deploys in slightly different forms in the *Republic* and again much later, in the course of an explicit examination of the claims of philosophical hedonism, in the *Philebus*. This is to the effect that the amount of pleasure that we *seem* to derive from the gratification of desire is greatly enhanced by contrast with the disagreeable condition of unsatisfied desire. The pleasure of gratification can therefore be regarded as comparable to the relief we get when a pain stops. It is something one very much wants, but something which can be seen, in a cool hour, to make a small contribution to well-being. It is to be contrasted with true pleasures, which are the things that give us pleasure when they come upon us unawares, like a pleasant scent that hits one unexpectedly, and which are therefore valued for their own sakes and not to any extent by contrast with the stress of some appetite which they relieve. Such true pleasures are not to be found in the sphere of carnal gratifications. This line of thought is well adapted to explain why the vulgar pleasures are grossly over-valued by the vulgar, and it can therefore be used in the game of trumping the vulgar hedonist. There is no doubt also that Plato did feel it necessary in the *Republic* to argue that the pursuit of justice does not entail the sacrifice of one's own well-being, and made use of the line of thought we have just mentioned to enable him to do so.

What is disputable is why he thought it necessary to argue this, whether because without such an argument he thought he could not persuade those of coarser fibre, or because he thought that there was some logical connection between goodness and happiness. In the *Laws*[1] he mentions this question, but does not answer it definitively. (The Athenian Stranger who conducts the discussion, has a low view of the philosophical grasp of his two companions). He displays, however, a strong preference for the view that there are not two distinct ways of life, the righteous and the agreeable, so related that the question could, logically, arise which of them a man was more to be congratulated for choosing. He asks what there is which could be a good to the righteous man and which is devoid of pleasure—are not honour

---

[1] *Laws* 662–3.

and renown agreeable, and the doing and suffering of no wrong? He observes shrewdly that parents want their children to be happy and tell them to be good, as if by complying with the latter they will realize the former. And he is clear about the propaganda value of the doctrine that the righteous life and the agreeable life are identical. Later[1] he seems to say that the righteous life is supreme not only in comeliness, but also in providing what we all desire, or that this is so if we are not allowed to turn away from the good life in childhood.

It is likely that Plato's views on this matter were not fully coherent. Both *goodness* and *pleasantness* are concepts the logical handling of which needs circumspection and sophistication. Plato sometimes seems to argue (in the *Gorgias* and the *Philebus*) against the identification of goodness and pleasantness by saying that we cannot suppose that the more pleasure a man is enjoying the better he is. If this is intended to refute the view that the goodness of the good life is logically bound up with its pleasurability, it seems to overlook the complexity of the concepts it is employing. If I say that what makes some way of life the best is that it is the most agreeable, I do imply that pleasure is the supreme value, but I still do not have to say that if Smith is, at the moment, happier than Brown, this means that Smith is, at the moment, a better man than Brown. Even if Smith is fortunate throughout his life, and Brown unfortunate, I still do not have to say that Smith is the better man, and I shall not do so if he has followed what is *in general* the less rewarding life. For it is what is in general less rewarding that is less to be recommended.

It is in itself unlikely that the first man to have tried to find his way through these tricky channels should never have grounded his boat. But if Plato never achieved a fully lucid view of these matters, it is probable that he sometimes at any rate must have felt inclined to say that there is some sort of logical connection between goodness and pleasurability. We have seen that the Athenian Stranger in the *Laws* favours the view that there is at least a *de facto* connection between the way of life which is most laudable and that which is most agreeable; but there are considerations which are likely to have tempted Plato to think that this is more than a happy coincidence. It is a fairly obvious idea that the function of pleasure and pain in the

[1] *Laws* 733.

scheme of things is to guide animals into the right sorts of activity and to keep them away from the wrong sorts. We have seen that the reason why we have carnal desires is in order that this may dispose us to take care of the body's needs; these desires, therefore, and their associated pleasures are designed to make us do things we otherwise would not trouble to do. It seems that Eudoxus, a member of Plato's circle, put forward the view that nature uses the reins of pleasure and pain to steer her creatures in the right way; and it is probably this view that Philebus is represented as maintaining in the dialogue named after him. It must have been difficult for Plato to avoid the view (which Aristotle subsequently crystallized) that pleasure is what happens when things are functioning as they should, pain what happens when a propensity is impeded. If you believe, or if your ancestors for centuries have believed, in original sin, you will be inclined to think that a human propensity is as likely to be bad as it is to be good. But if you believe that men and other animals only exist as ordered systems, because an intelligible pattern has been imposed upon disorderly material, then you will be inclined to think that every drive which exists in the animal is an attempt on the part of the pattern to assert itself; and with this picture you will surely be inclined to think that things go smoothly only in so far as they go rightly, and that stress is always due to resistance offered by the material to the self-assertion of the intelligible pattern. This will make you very inclined to think that pleasure is the sign that things are going in the way nature intends, pain the sign that they are going otherwise. Since you are unlikely to regard as reasonable the view that there might be for you a pattern of life superior to that which creative reason had in mind in designing the kind of organism of which you are an instance, you are likely to believe that pleasure is what you feel when you are living rightly, pain what you feel when things are happening to you that ought not to be happening. Some of these things of course will be morally irrelevant; damage to you by another animal in a fight is something that ought not to happen, and it will be painful, but it may not be your fault. Correspondingly things may give you pleasure for which you deserve no credit; and certain things will give momentary pleasure even when they are indulged out of season. Being an imperfectly rational creature you will tend to shun short-term pains and pursue short-term pleasures; and things may work out so that in the end you do not pay a very heavy price for doing so; you may be lucky, luckier than Smith who has much pain imposed upon him by external circumstances, and very little pleasure beyond what comes from his rectitude. In the limiting case in which external circumstances are most perversely stacked, a man who lives badly may suffer less, perhaps, than a man who lives well but has consistent bad luck. But one will still be tempted to argue that good and bad fortune fall at random on the just and on the unjust, that what happens *within* a man is in general more decisive of happiness and unhappiness than what happens *to* him, and that therefore the good life will be in general happier than any other.

This does not mean of course that we ought to pursue pleasure, and that the man who thinks most about his own happiness is the most laudable. It means that the pursuit of happiness is natural and innocent, and that a morality which tries to impose upon all of us a way of life, by which in general each man who follows it has to sacrifice his own well-being, must be wrong. This is a position which the *Republic* seems to take for granted, and it is a less extreme position than that which seems to be toyed with in the *Protagoras* according to which it is the pleasantness of the good life which makes it good. It allows there to exist an independent criterion of goodness, namely accordance with the dispositions of creative reason. That Plato should have puzzled over the relationship between pleasure and goodness, and favoured different answers at different times seems entirely likely. The *Protagoras* suggests that plain men only denounce an attractive course as wrong if they implicitly believe it to be unattractive in the long run; and it seems to play with the idea that all that we need in order to live rightly is an explicit adoption of this method of determining moral issues—it suggests that a knowledge how to measure pleasure would be "the salvation of life". The *Phaedo* on the other hand makes Socrates denounce the idea that calculation of pleasures and pains plays any part in the moral outlook of the philosopher. It is his single-minded love of wisdom that simply makes everything that is incompatible with this pursuit distasteful to him. He hates cowardice or self-indulgence because these are disordered conditions, not because they do not pay in the end. We gather from Aristotle that these questions were much disputed in the Academy, Eudoxus leading the hedonists, Speusippus their opponents. It seems likely that Plato wrote the *Philebus* in order to intervene in this dispute. In this dialogue he shows some sympathy with the view of Eudoxus, at least to the extent that he takes for granted that the question is: "Which way of life is the most *eudaimôn*?"—a word which can be translated "happy", but which means perhaps something more like "blessed" or "worthy of emulation". He shows also some, rather guarded, sympathy with Speusippus' view that pleasure and pain are both processes, pleasure being what happens when things are getting better, pain what happens when they are getting worse; and that therefore the ideal life will contain neither pleasure nor pain, since a perfect state, once achieved, is stable, and will get neither better nor worse. He is clear, however, that such a condition is outside human range. But what Plato seems to want to say to the contending parties is that the good life must be both consistent with the demands of intelligence and also satisfying to us, and that of these two criteria the first is much more important than the second. This means, in the spirit of the *Laws*, that the most righteous life is the most agreeable, and that this could not be otherwise because we could not accept a life which was not agreeable. Its pleasantness, therefore, is a necessary condition of the goodness of the good life, but it is not its essence.

A digression may be convenient at this point. Hedonism is often thought to be a selfish doctrine. This is not necessarily correct. The hedonist believes that it is natural, right, perhaps inevitable that a man should pursue his own well-being; but he can perfectly well also believe that a man can only achieve his own well-being if he selflessly concerns himself with that of others. Plato seems to have believed something rather less than this. Charity was not a Greek virtue; neglect of one's own rights beyond a certain point tended to be a sign of weakness. Nor was it my duty to concern myself overmuch with the spiritual welfare of others. The virtuous man as we see him in Plato and in Aristotle is a man who makes no undue demands on others, who is hospitable, courteous, generous, though not till it hurts;

he has friends, and for them he will go to greater lengths than for others. But on the whole he cultivates a certain self-sufficiency. Our business is to make ourselves noble. This entails respect for the rights of others, and affection towards friends and family. Except on the field of battle it is not likely to entail much self-sacrifice.

Except perhaps in the *Protagoras* Plato never sponsors the view that we can decide what we ought to do by asking what course is in general and in the long run the pleasantest. By the time of the *Laws* certainly, and probably before, he had become too well aware that what we enjoy depends in part on what we are familiar with to say that. For the man who has been badly brought up, and is therefore corrupt, will find his corrupt things familiar, and his answer to the question "Which course is the pleasantest?" will be the wrong one. It may be that what is congenial to the corrupt man is in some absolute sense less pleasant that what is congenial to the uncorrupt man (the *Republic* seems to want to maintain this), but this is something that the corrupt man cannot know; for if he were philosopher enough to see the reasoning which bring us to this conclusion (if he knew that bodily pleasures owe much of their apparent pleasantness to the fact that they relieve the stress of appetite, and other things of this kind), then he would not be a corrupt man. Pleasantness, therefore, is not a useful criterion of rightness, since only the philosopher can use it safely, and he does not need it.

How then does Plato think that we do or should determine how to live and what to do? The philosopher presumably does this in the light of his knowledge of what a human being is and of the conditions under which human life is lived. The *Republic* suggests that the rest of us will be wise to accept the guidance of the philosophers. Since Plato knew that philosophers in this sense do not commonly exist, this perhaps means that he would have said that we ought to follow the advice of the best and wisest men we could find—though he would undoubtedly have accompanied this with some fairly sharp observations about the ways in which poets and other sages acquire a reputation for wisdom. Perhaps on the other hand some of us can try to be our own philosophers, following the train of thought that these mythical beings would follow, as Plato himself followed it in the *Republic*.

But there is also a strongly "aesthetic" element in Plato's conception of the good life. The word *kalon* is the Greek both for "noble" and for "beautiful", and to many Greeks nobility of life was a kind of beauty, beauty a kind of nobility. The conception of order and harmony was probably for Plato the common source both of aesthetic and of ethical standards. He often emphasizes the inter-relatedness of aesthetics and ethics. In one place in the *Laws* he says that we are the gods' playthings, and our duty is to make our play as comely as we can. Life is not serious business interspersed with recreation; our obligation is to produce beauty, in our leisure as much as in our business activities. Leisure indeed has the greater dignity because it is this which can be beautified. The good life, therefore, is the beautiful life; and this is the same as to say that it is the life which commends itself to reason, and therefore to the only thing in us which has any single direction. Whatever in us is not a drive towards order and harmony is either a falling back into chaos and indeterminacy, or else it is a pursuit beyond the due limit of one of the manifold propensities each of which has its place in the ordered life and each of which can generate disorder if it is followed too single-mindedly. Therefore, while the impulse to the good life is unitary and coherent, our contrary impulses are all at war with each other; and he who pursues harmony in his life can be reasonably sure that he is living as he should. Certainly our inherent impulse towards order and harmony is disrupted by the shock of incarnation, and by the stream of "sense-perceptions" which serve to interpret to us the alien physical world we are obliged to sojourn in. But this impulse remains, and the concern of education is to strengthen it. It can be strengthened by every element of beauty and harmony with which a child can be surrounded; and, as it is strengthened, it develops into a propensity to create these qualities wherever possible. The conduct of life is pre-eminently a field in which this can be done. A potter shaping a pot and a man shaping his conduct are doing analogous things; and familiarity with shapely pots will contribute its mite towards strengthening a man's love of beauty and therefore his desire to beautify his life.

Virtue and the Pursuit of Happiness

Therefore a man whose education has been conducted as it should be will be found to have a distaste for whatever in life is ugly and disorderly and a love for whatever has the beauty of coherence. This is stressed both in the *Republic* and in the *Laws*; and in both dialogues it is also said that this quasi-aesthetic moral response, while it is the best that most men can have, is insufficient on its own; for it is insufficient for those who have to take decisions of principle, and in particular for those who have to determine the form which education and cultural activities should take in a world whose traditional patterns have been broken. The activities in which culture consists—rhythmic movement in dancing or poetry, harmony in music, and the like—are natural expressions of the human soul, and they can all be done clumsily or elegantly. But in addition to this that which they express can be good or bad; music can express the dignity of moral striving or the effeminacy of precious leisure. It is vital, therefore, that the right guidance should be given to those who determine our cultural patterns, and for this, philosophic insight into the nature of the good life is required.

That evil conduct is distasteful to the man in whom the inherent love of harmony is strong is no doubt part of what made Plato say that the life of virtue is the happiest life; that is to say, part of what he intends by this is that vicious activities are repugnant to the virtuous. Cowardice is "more to be feared" than wounds and death not only because the life which coward-ice brings with it contains more of the things that we all seek to shun, but also because, from the viewpoint of the good man (and, as Aristotle asks, what other should one adopt?), it is quite simply unattractive.

What degree of freedom does Plato suppose we have in the moral life? With regard to the question what pattern of life we ought to aim at, our freedom is certainly limited. There is in one sense only one good life, the life which expresses the successful reassertion of our impulse towards harmony, and which involves, therefore, the smooth co-ordination of all our other impulses and of our social relationships. The good life will be, among other things, the social life and must therefore manifest the social and civic virtues. In principle this is not as constricting as it may sound. The proposition that there is only one good life, namely that which is orderly and coherent for man as a social creature, leaves plenty of room for creativity. There are many different ways of realizing in concrete form the direction to live coherently as a social creature; moralists who bridle at the notion that there is only one good life seldom really demand more diversity than this theoretically allows. Most of us, however, demand more diversity than Plato in practice allows. Undeniably he tended towards intolerance, and towards the view that there is just one best way, in concrete, of doing each thing. In spite of his sharp criticisms of the poets and of other traditional sages, and in spite of the radicalism which he sometimes displayed towards traditional institutions (for example his criticism of the family as an institution unfit for philosophers in the *Republic*), he shows a marked sympathy for traditional ideas, and is very unwilling to entertain novel conceptions such as, for instance, that a gentleman might fittingly indulge in useful productive labour. Or again while he is sometimes very enlightened in his attitude to foreigners, ridiculing the division of mankind into Greeks and barbarians, he never seems to regard it as a really open question whether forms of political organization other than the city-state might have any virtue. He tends in practice to demand much more conformity to traditional Greek ideals (admittedly an eclectic selection from those of Sparta as well as Athens) than he theoretically needed to demand.

What, however, of moral freedom in the sense of the controversy between libertarians and determinists? To what extent did he think that we are actually able to choose how to act? The free-will controversy in its modern form has to some extent theological origins. One of the issues is whether wrong moral choices have an unbroken causal ancestry going back to the moment of creation, and whether, therefore, we must impute to the creator some responsibility for the evil that men do. This issue would not have presented itself to Plato in this form; evil for him could always be imputed to the deficiencies of the medium in which creative reason had to work. I doubt if the question whether we can think of human choices as caused ever presented itself to him as a question which needed to be asked. He certainly does not think, however, that we can impute to

God, or to the universe, the responsibility for our evil choices. Such a view would be inconsistent with what seems to be his conception of responsibility. He tends to regard praise and blame, reward and punishment as stimuli designed to make us exert the moral effort that we ought to exert and are rightly censured for failing to exert. He tends to think that a just punishment is one that benefits the victim by purging out of him, through suffering, the evil tendencies which made him act as he did. It is a form of spiritual therapy—though he has greater faith in the therapeutic value of suffering than most of us can manage nowadays. In so far as we are curable by censure we are responsible.

On the other hand he also tends to think that, although we ought to exert moral effort against our impulses and can be censured if we fail to do so, nevertheless a man cannot choose what seems to him the less attractive of two courses. We find this view not only in the *Protagoras*; there are traces of it also in, for example, the *Laws*. Plato retains, throughout, sympathy with Socrates' paradox that no man deliberately does what he sees to be wrong, and draws the corollary that we should pity evil-doers (even if we have to treat them with severity) since their evil-doing must have proceeded from an inability to see the better course as better. Failure, also, to see something as the better course remains closely related to failure to see it as the more attractive course. The word for "good" (*agathon*) never loses the connotation "desirable", and Plato never divorces, as a Kantian would wish to do, finding X laudable from finding X desirable. If (as we have seen) he never tells us quite clearly why he thinks that laudability and desirability must go hand in hand, nevertheless he persists in believing this. Therefore he lays great emphasis (especially in the *Laws*) on the importance of inculcating right tastes and preferences. If the man is to act rightly, the boy must be made to learn to like doing the things which his duty will require of him. He must be made to like doing sober and courageous actions and dislike doing the opposite. As we have seen, the effect upon him of "harmony" in his educational environment tends in this direction; but this must of course be reinforced by actual practice of the actions in which virtue consists. Martial music will help to inculcate disdain for cowardice, but martial exercises will stiffen the influence.

Virtue and the Pursuit of Happiness

There are two levels on which the love of virtue can operate, the level of reason and that of spirit. The *Republic* argues that the influence of the more "cultural" sides of education (music, dancing and the like) is to produce a love of virtue on the rational level; that of the more "athletic" sides is to produce a love of virtue on the spirited level. Moral attitudes involve an intellectual and an affective element; we judge things to be right or wrong, and we feel admiration or disdain for them. The judgment is something which operates on the level of the rational element. It is a recognition, implicit or explicit, of the presence or absence of order and harmony in the course to which it relates; and it is at this point that the influence of order and harmony upon us is effective. Admiration and disdain are the typical expression of the spirited element in personality, and the direction which they take in the adult are vastly affected by what he has been taught to admire and disdain in his youth. Formal training is not the only influence which acts at this level (the *Republic* has some shrewd observations on the tendency of children to watch what happens to their parents and draw their own conclusions); but it remains a powerful influence.

No man, then, can choose the less attractive of two courses. What for some men makes the right course more attractive is their conscious, single-minded love of wisdom and their contempt for whatever is irrelevant to this pursuit, for whatever is trivial, conventional, based upon the ends that men do pursue but that the philosopher can see to be not worth pursuing. For other men the ability to find the right course more attractive is due to the conditioning effect upon them of environment and training in making effective in their minds the considerations which the philosopher explicitly recognizes, in tempering their emotional responses so that they feel admiration and disdain for the right things, and in curbing the over-development of emotions and desires which can very easily take place if we are permitted to indulge these beyond due limits. Evil-doing is always to be traced to the usurpation of an undue share in determining the course of a man's life by a propensity, whether of the spirited or of the appetitive element in personality, which ought to play a subordinate part. The man who is arrogant and aggressive is the man in whom self-respect does not play its

Virtue and the Pursuit of Happiness

natural part (which is to protect him from the illegitimate encroachment upon him of other men or of his own desires), but has assumed the guiding role. The man who is luxury-loving and self-indulgent is similarly a slave of desire. Culture in the widest sense is for most of us the only defence against such usurpations; and if the culture of our community is corrupt, nothing but a "divine dispensation" can save us.

12

Culture and the Imagination

ONE hears a good deal about Plato's philosophy of art. It is not clear to me that he had anything that deserves to be called a philosophy of art. He had a philosophy of culture, as we have seen, and this had repercussions on the liberty that he thought artists should enjoy; but that is a rather different matter. There are, however, remarks in various places about such topics as beauty and the arts which can perhaps be strung together and made something of.

Among contemporary aestheticians, those who sign on under the slogan "Art for art's sake" tend to think that it is the business of the artist to create concrete expressions of emotional and other responses or attitudes to life, or to fragments of life. They tend also to think that the great artist is the man who has novel responses and who can enable us to share them by expressing them in a work of art. One sometimes wonders whether those who say this sort of thing about "art" in general have not concentrated unduly on the literary arts. If we are to suppose that Plato would have committed himself to observations about art in general, then perhaps we could accuse him of concentrating insufficiently on the literary arts. Certainly the notion that the artist is primarily engaged upon freezing into objective form a transient human response is not a notion that seems to have occurred to him.

The artist is for Plato primarily the man who tries to impose certain formal qualities (harmony for short) upon things that men are naturally disposed to make or do. We have a natural propensity towards "movement of the voice and limbs"[1]—

[1] *Laws* Book 2.

towards singing and dancing—and, unlike other animals, a natural ability to perceive and to enjoy organization, rhythm and harmony in these things. What the Greeks called "music" (including dancing and poetry, much of which was written to be chanted or sung) derives from these natural propensities. Similar remarks no doubt apply to the imposition of organization, rhythm and harmony by the potter, sculptor and the like. There is, however, more than one kind of organization rhythm and harmony. One sort of harmony "imitates" (i.e. has an affinity with) one sort of moral character. A work of art can fail either because it is incompetently done, or because, though competently done and therefore possessed of harmony, the harmony which it has is a base kind of harmony. A beautiful work of art is presumably one which has the noblest kind of harmony, skilfully imposed. Such works excite and deserve an aesthetic response, and, as we have seen, have a good influence on character.

Beauty is also a characteristic not only of organized wholes but of elements. We learn in the *Philebus* that pure shapes and sounds, individually as well as in composition, are beautiful and excite what Plato calls pure pleasure. The theory is perhaps that there is in man an innate tendency to respond with pleasure both to what is pure, simple and unmixed, and also to whatever is harmoniously organized. It is not difficult to recognize these qualities—simplicity and organization—as qualities in which reason is interested, and we can conjecture fairly confidently that the delight which we take in whatever has these qualities is the delight which reason takes in finding these qualities in the physical world. Aesthetic appreciation will thus be at bottom the same thing as moral approval in that both will be responses to *to kalon*, "the noble-beautiful", which is identical with *to agathon* "the good", "the worth-pursuing", in that nothing is worth pursuing but what reason endorses, and in that reason endorses nothing but what is simple, or orderly, or both.

The connection between aesthetic appreciation and the interests of reason emerges in an unexpected place, namely in Plato's theory of sexual attraction as it is outlined in the *Symposium* and the *Phaedrus*. Beautiful bodies are examples of beautiful things; they are presumably instances of organized harmony. The sight of a beautiful thing excites us, as we saw, and in particular excites in the rational element in the soul a memory of its true home. This excitement is particularly intense where the beautiful thing is a fellow human being. The soul has a vivid memory, as the *Phaedrus* puts it, of beauty as it saw it in its purity before it descended into the body; it is elevated above its normal identification with mundane considerations, thus becoming "mad", though with the divine madness of *erôs* or romantic love; and it reaches out after immortality. Because, presumably, of the exigencies of procreation this madness has been associated with the desire for intercourse. This desire is of course legitimate when the purpose is to beget children: but this way of achieving immortality, by leaving progeny in the world, is not the noblest use of *erôs*. Its noblest use (and Plato assumes that this will only arise in platonic homosexual relations between males) is when it makes its victims strive after immortality through creative works of the mind, and when it leads lover and beloved into true friendship on the plane of philosophic discourse. (To have recommended romantic attachments which were nevertheless to be kept strictly platonic is perhaps a good example of Plato's strong streak of practical silliness. He might have done better if he had not taken for granted that no intellectual relationship between men and women is worth much).

So far, then, beautiful things are those which have the power to excite in us delight, this delight being of a noble kind; and this they do by manifesting the properties of simplicity and harmony which reason loves, and (if they are the kind of object which can express anything) by expressing or "imitating" noble activities and attitudes. Alongside objects such as these, which deserve to be called noble or beautiful, there are also objects, whose formal properties are coherent enough to render them expressive, but which succeed in expressing what is base. The rhythm and harmony—the ordered dance-like quality— which characterize any successful piece of poetry give it power over the imagination; but the power may be directed towards bad ends. The sentiments of the poet may be cowardly or otherwise unworthy. The musician and the sculptor do not speak in the direct sense in which the poet speaks; but their products too can express courage or cowardice, restraint or self-indulgence. It is obvious, therefore, that products even of the less representational arts can be criticized on moral as well as technical grounds.

You can condemn a dance or a tune for effeminacy, or praise it for martial dignity; and I suppose that you can find similar things to blame or praise in a poem, or a piece of sulpture, "(a Barbara Hepworth even, where no representational considerations arise, as they do with a Phidias)." In certain sorts of political community, therefore, you will expect the arts to be subject to political censorship.

In more than one place Plato says that poetry, like love, is a kind of madness; and he tells us that the poet must write under some kind of divine possession since he commonly has no rational knowledge of the subjects that he writes about. Creative ability in fact in the poet is a gift whereby the poet is able to conjure up an imaginative atmosphere. In describing a battle he can create the atmosphere of battle, can make us feel we are taking part in one; and he can do all this without having any understanding of warfare. Likewise the painter can bring before us a blacksmith's forge, can make us smell the singed hoof and hear the ring of the anvil; and he can do this without knowing so much as what the bellows are for. It is this power on the part of the creative artist that made Plato deliver his well-known polemic against representational artists, and poets in particular, in the tenth book of the *Republic*. The attack comes in two waves. The first wave is directed against the status commonly allowed to the poet and his colleagues. Because Homer can recreate so miraculously what it is like to be present at a battle, or to sit at counsel with men of heroic stature, we feel that he must know about these things. Therefore, we take Homer and other poets as guides to life. (The Greeks in Plato's time appear to have done this to a considerable extent. The hackneyed statement that Homer was the Bible of the Greeks is true enough if we assume that Plato's contemporaries were post-Darwinians). But there is no justification for doing this. A man who can paint a convincing picture of a bed—who can recreate what it is like to be in the presence of a bed—need not in order to do so know what a bed really is, in the way in which a user of a bed knows what a bed really is; he need not even have the right ideas about what a bed ought to be like, as a carpenter can come to have the right ideas on such a matter by consulting the user. All he needs to have is a gift for creating a likeness. And the same is true of a poet.

Representational artists make reproductions of reproductions; that is all they have to be able to do, and it is quite a different skill from the skill of making reproductions of realities, and different again from understanding realities. In the case of a bed the reality is the function of a bed, the form of which beds are instances. Actual beds are "reproductions" of this, and pictures of beds are reproductions of these reproductions. Carpenters *quâ* carpenters do not know what beds ought to be like—that is the prerogative of those who sleep on them; and painters need to know even less, because they do not receive instructions from the user as the carpenter does. Analogously (I think) generals *quâ* generals do not have to understand what war is about, but merely how to make an efficient job of it. Understanding what war is about is the prerogative of those who have the art of statesmanship, the art which uses the skill of generals to achieve results when these results are seen to be desirable—in other words it is the prerogative of philosophers. This prerogative is not to be usurped by poets, whose skill in recreating what it is like to be a general on the field of battle gives them even less understanding than the generals possess of the issues at stake.

Plato has paid a heavy penalty for writing this passage and for allowing Socrates to debunk Homer by making a dead-pan comparison of him to a painter painting a picture of a bed. He has been accused of believing in the unreality of actual beds compared with that of the Bed which God made, and other things which can indeed be extracted from his language if it is taken quite seriously. However that may be, this is the first wave in the attack on representational art, and its effect is to show that the ability to recreate appearances is valueless. At the best it could be allowed to be a harmless amusement. It does not follow of course that the medium through which the representation is conveyed—the pattern of words or the shaped marble—is valueless. This presumably could still manifest formal qualities of an admirable kind and could perhaps even be beautiful if people would attend to its formal qualities rather than admire it for the cunning of the representation it conveys. (Plato does not actually make this point—it would hardly have helped him with the criticism of Homer that he is currently engaged on—and I do not of course know how readily he would have admitted it). The second wave of the attack, however, tries to show that representational art is not only valueless in practice but also pernicious. In the case of visual art the reason is, perhaps rather half-heartedly, that interest in representation encourages our already excessive propensity to concern ourselves with the look of things. In the case of poetry the charge is that, since the depiction of virtue is uninteresting (Plato is thinking by now primarily of the drama), the poet portrays vice; and since the sober portrayal of anything is unexciting, the poet portrays everything in emotionally violent terms. Our propensity towards uncontrolled emotion and generally undignified, effeminate behaviour is therefore greatly nourished by attendance at the theatre and by indulgence in poetry.

These puritanical half-truths are not repeated elsewhere; I do not know how seriously Plato meant us to take them, or to what extent he may have been amusing himself by sticking pins into Homer and the tragedians. What is, however, without doubt entirely serious is the doctrine that whatever powerfully moves the imagination has a powerful effect on character, that therefore the artist cannot be exempt from the philosopher's criticism; and also that the artist's gifts are of a non-rational kind, a matter of *enthousiasmos* or "divine possession", akin to the madness of love and totally distinct from the apprehension of truth. Understanding is achieved by rational methods, by prose, by mathematics. There may be an intuitive element in understanding, in that the final apprehension of rational principles may go beyond the capacity to formulate them in propositions. But there is no inspirational element, and the business of the artist is to create beauty, not to compete with the philosopher in the understanding of truth. Indeed he must accept the rulings of the philosopher as to what effects upon the imagination he may and may not exercise. As the doctor in his capacity as doctor is skilled in creating certain effects and not in knowing whether they are desirable, so it is with the artist in his capacity as artist. As in other spheres, if he is a man of noble character bad imaginative effects will be repugnant to him; but in the end it is for the philosopher to say whether or not the influence of a given artist is pernicious.

13

The Good Society

THE part that Plato himself played in public affairs ought to tell us something about his attitude to politics. If we can accept (with the bulk of scholarly opinion) the authenticity of certain of the letters allegedly written by Plato, particularly the Seventh, we can form a sufficiently clear picture of his career. There is nothing impossible in the notion that the letters are forged. The Seventh Letter, however, contains a long philosophical digression; and while a forger, who wished to exert some influence or other on Syracusan affairs by a document purporting to come from Plato, might have included a philosophical digression for the sake of verisimilitude, it has to be said that this particular forger has gone to the trouble of providing quite an unnecessarily lengthy and complicated piece of philosophy. You and I would have put in something shorter and simpler. We should also have put in something less original; considered as a forger's work the Seventh Letter is oddly un-Platonic. If Plato himself wrote it, after the time of the *Theaetetus*, it is not difficult to see why he says what he says—why he says, for example, at one point, that the difference between knowledge and right belief is unimportant in the present context.[1] But a forger who wrote that and expected to get away with it was a bold man. You and I would have kept closer to things for which we could find scriptural warrant in the dialogues.

If we assume then that we can accept the authenticity of the Seventh Letter and of certain of the others, we can say something along the following lines. As a young man Plato held aloof

1 EPD 2, pp. 122–7.

from the oligarchical conspiracies which took place towards the time of Athens' final defeat in the Peloponnesian War—though some of those involved in them were relatives of his and had been associated with Socrates. Socrates himself refused to get involved in certain of their lawless activities. When the democracy was restored, however, it proceeded to get rid of Socrates, bringing against him a charge of impiety, but actually no doubt regarding him as a dangerous critic of established democratic practices, and one who was too much involved with oligarchical adventurers. Plato had been at any rate fairly closely associated with Socrates, and had to remove to Megara for a while. At some stage he returned to Athens where, he says, he waited and watched for opportunities of political action, but found himself unable to do anything; action needs friends and associates, and he could not, owing to the breakdown of the ancestral way of life, find anybody to join with him in doing the things he wanted to do. So he became disillusioned with democratic politics, and came to the conclusion that the human race would never cease from travail until true philosophers held political power, or those in power turned in earnest to philosophy. Thereafter he tends to think of ruling as something which is or can be done by one man, and to be prepared to use of this man the unpopular word *basileus* or "king".

Ten years after Socrates' death Plato visited Syracuse. Syracuse at this time was ruled by a tyrant Dionysius I, a tough military autocrat. (A "tyrant" in this context means a sort of South American president, not necessarily a brutal or unjust despot, and probably in some sense a "man of the people"). Plato was shocked at the luxury and licence of the Syracusans, but became friendly with Dionysius' brother-in-law Dion. Plato did not stay in Syracuse very long—there are various stories about why he left and what happened to him—but returned to Athens and in due course, one supposes, founded the Academy, which occupied most of his energies for the rest of his life. Some twenty years after his first Syracusan visit, however, Dionysius I died and was succeeded by his son Dionysius II. Dion appears to have felt that his nephew the new tyrant was an impressionable man and that Plato could do something with him. Plato went to Syracuse and tried to do what he could. He seems to have acted or tried to act as tutor as well as mentor to the young ruler. Dionysius was given a sort of summary account of the topics he would have to study if he became Plato's pupil. It does not seem to have made him want to occupy that status, but he appears to have been glad to have Plato around. Others, however, were jealous of Plato's influence; there were factions, there was a democratic party. Dionysius seems to have lashed out in various ways to preserve his authority; and Syracusan affairs became chaotic for two decades, until after Plato's death. Plato left Syracuse with difficulty after about two years, returned later and had to be extricated once more, thereafter remaining in touch with Syracusan affairs from a distance. Whatever Plato hoped to achieve in Syracuse, his hopes cannot have been realized.

One can tell this story in various ways. An aristocratic Athenian, implicated with oligarchical conspirators, but too cautious to burn his fingers, bides his time in Athens, but his time never comes. Tired of waiting he abandons politics until an opportunity for power turns up in Syracuse. Or a vain young intellectual, angry at the way his birth and talents are ignored by the democracy, compensates for this neglect by conceiving the view that one can do nothing with the Athenians, until an opportunity comes for trying out his theories about government in Syracuse; foiled there by the refusal of human nature to conform to his *a priori* notions, he goes back to Athens, and climbs even higher up his ivory tower. Or a rather strait-laced young man coming from a slightly old-fashioned, puritanical home, endowed with poor practical judgment and an all-or-nothing way of looking at things; he tries to take up his civic responsibilities—he has a sense of duty to the community—but he cannot see how to bring about the things he wants to bring about, largely because he entirely lacks the politician's skill in estimating what step can feasibly be taken; baffled, he decides that the only thing to do is to try by education to build up a healthier public opinion. However, his sense of public duty makes him go to Syracuse when the existence of an apparently malleable young ruler makes it seem that something could perhaps be achieved in an outpost of Greek civilization which is sadly in need of reform.

It is useless to try to decide either between these stories, or in what proportions to blend them. But there are certain points that can be made. Firstly Plato was never, in theory or, it seems, in practice in favour of arbitrary rule. He praises "freedom" by which he seems to mean the ability to live one's life unmolested provided one abides by the rules. (There will be more rules, however, than we are accustomed to). Again he is not in favour of privilege. He distrusts wealth, hates the co-existence of wealth with poverty, and is as little in favour of an inegalitarian society as some of his severest critics. He does not favour the undivided authority of any but "philosophers", or those who have insight into the nature of things. In Syracuse he seems to have commended "constitutionalism". Though he is a totalitarian in that he holds that in principle a government of philosophers may lay down regulations governing the whole of life (he does not believe in "areas of individual decision", nor value non-conformity for its own sake), he is in no sense an *étatiste*, willing to concede a divine right to the established government just because it is established; nor has he any sympathy with blood, race or national glory theories. He is what we would call a little simple-minded about questions of political dynamics, though perhaps we ought to accompany that with the reminder that the study of these matters was in its infancy. Finally his sentiments were democratic in that there is nothing but superior knowledge which gives a man the right to superior political status; and he does not hold that such status carries with it the right to wealth or privilege, nor that those who are well-born are particularly likely to be gifted with superior knowledge. The democracy which he found it impossible to work in was not democracy as we know it. It was government by universal assembly; and Plato's quarrel with it is that it offered no safeguard whatever against the triumph of proposals which were foolish or immoral. Demagogy was irresistible in a popular assembly; somebody had only to suggest, with oratorical skill, an attractive course, however misguided or degenerate, for it to be accepted with acclamation. And Sophists existed who were willing to teach that oratorical skill to any gifted young man. Probably Plato was mistaken in this estimate of Athenian democracy; probably the Athenians were more sensible than either he or Socrates realized. The truth may be that neither of them understood the gradual and frustrating nature of progress in public affairs, and that both of them were too inclined to treat every set-back to common sense as the final triumph of folly. But what Plato seems to have wanted was something that modern democratic systems provide, and that government by assembly does not provide, namely institutions which put a premium on caution and good sense and enable these to hold out against the swings of public opinion.

Plato's best known contribution to political thought is the *Republic*. The political theory of the *Republic* is really very simple. We begin by observing that there are three functions to be discharged in every community:—decision-making or ruling; enforcement of the law by police-action against law-breakers and by military action against foreign enemies; and the production of goods. (It is suggested that the first two functions could be dispensed with in a community of self-disciplined ascetics; but those who are determined to have comfort are determined to have the things which create conflict between individuals and within each man, and which also lead to demands for territorial expansion. Such men, therefore, must be governed, policed and equipped with an army). Only a small number of men are capable of ruling wisely; and by no means everybody can be trusted to use military force both courageously and also with restraint. The first two functions, therefore, are specialist functions. In a rationally ordered community, therefore, men would be chosen to rule, and to man the army, on the strength of intellectual, moral and physical fitness; and productive activities would be left to the remainder. On the assumption that a man does his job best if he has only one job to do, we should see to it that the rulers ruled, the soldiers trained and fought, and the workers worked, and that nobody interfered with anybody else's function.

That is really all there is to it; ruling is a specialist function and should, ideally, be left to those competent to discharge it. Since they are competent, and since also, as a class set apart, maintained at public expense and with no part in economic activity, they are disinterested, they will rule justly, having no temptation to do otherwise. Their subordinates, therefore, will have no grounds for complaint, and will soon learn to see that it is better to get on with one's own private affairs and not get involved in politics. Because such a community is sensibly organized it will be happy and peaceful; and there is no other way in which such a state of affairs can come about. That is the abstract political theory of the *Republic*.

Plato takes the opportunity, however, to string on to this theme a good many things that he wants to say about the assumptions under which public affairs are conducted. Socrates is made to give a rough outline of a city constructed on such principles. He tells us something of the education, intellectual and physical, which he will give to the young candidates for the status of "guardians" or rulers, and "auxiliaries" or soldiers. He sketches a system of tests, intellectual and physical, by which people are to be selected and reselected at various ages for these two responsible functions. Plato's views on literature and the arts, on moral education, on the nature of virtue are worked into this account. The question of the nature of virtue is got into the story by means of an analogy which Socrates draws between the three classes in his imaginary community and the three elements in individual personality. The rulers correspond to the rational element, the soldiers to the spirited, the producers to the appetitive. This does not mean, as has sometimes been supposed, that the rulers are the only wise men in the city, the soldiers the only brave men, and the producers the luxury-loving and lascivious remainder. The analogy holds between functions; just as it is the business of our rationality to guide our lives, of our self-respect to stiffen our resolution, and of our carnal desires to ensure that we nourish ourselves and reproduce our kind, so it is the business of the rulers to rule, of the soldiers to use what force is needed, and of the producers to keep the community alive and comfortable. But everybody, whichever class he belongs to, will need every virtue. A specially wise man will in practice be spotted and trained to rule, a specially brave man who is not particularly intelligent will be allocated to the army; and a man of poor moral fibre will have no option but to produce; or rather these allocations will be provisionally made in childhood and confirmed, or otherwise, later on. But this does not mean that there will be no sensible, brave and temperate men among the producers; the system only works on the assumption that most of them have these qualities. Otherwise they would rebel no doubt against the cultural and other provisions which are intended to preserve and enhance them.

Socrates goes on to tell us of the manner of life of his rulers and their auxiliaries. (He does not make it very clear how much of what he says applies to both classes and how much only to the rulers). They are to live an austere life in barracks, maintained at the public expense. Women are eligible for membership of the ruling class and of the army just as much as men. There is to be no marriage nor family life. Breeding will take place at stated intervals between couples selected so far as possible on eugenic grounds. The children will be taken away from their parents and reared in state nurseries, never to know who their parents were. Thus all of those who were conceived at the same festival will be each other's "brothers" and "sisters", and it is suggested that this widening of the boundaries of the "family" will enable public spirit to supplant clan-loyalties.

The further education of the rulers, the education designed to enable them to take decisions of principle, is formidable. It consists of mathematics and philosophy, and lasts till the age of thirty-five. The mathematics (which occupies ten years of the course) is intended, I think, to set before those, who are subsequently to be made to philosophize, images of the forms the nature of which they will have to try to understand. The theory is, as we saw, that every rational principle has its embodiment in the field of mathematics as well as in the organization of physical things. At the age of thirty-five the future rulers go off to fifteen years' military and government service, and then at the age of fifty are brought back to be conducted to the vision of goodness. Thereafter they take their turn at ruling, spending the rest of their time in intellectual activity. What they actually do when they rule is not very clear. Socrates goes into no details of the legal code of his imaginary city except for those parts of it which determine the selection, upbringing and manner of life of his ruling classes, and the censorship of cultural activities which they will impose. The rest of the legal code, he suggests will more or less arrange itself once the basic structure of the community is sound. They will not, therefore, be much engaged in legislation. Plato always tended to think that the legislative problem was simply to get the laws right once and for all, and then maintain the *status quo*. That social evolution might require continual modification of even the best legal code is an idea that does not seem to have occurred to him. We must suppose, then, that the rulers spend most of their time during their tours of duty in more or less judicial activities, and in supervising and censoring education and culture so that all the influences which play upon the imagination are healthy.

How serious is Plato about all this? There is no doubt that he is entirely serious over the point that no community can flourish unless those who understand the moral issues on which good government depends are allowed to govern and to determine the cultural influences. But did he seriously think that such a community could ever come into existence? On more detailed matters, did he believe that there could exist a governing class maintained in barracks at public expense, deprived of family life, forbidden to own wealth? Or are these proposals intended as satiric criticism of the assumptions of Athenian life? When he says that his rulers are to be allowed no contact with gold, is he to be taken literally, or is he making the same point as Sir Thomas More when he says that in Utopia only bedroom utensils are made of this metal? Is he, that is, simply ridiculing the ordinary scale of values?

It is difficult to answer these questions with any confidence. One feels tempted to say that no one could have supposed that a bit of *a priori* thought was capable of telling him just in what way social life could most profitably be taken to bits and put together again. But then one remembers Lenin for example and Mao-Tse-Tung, men whose dreams have been as radical as Plato's, and who have ventured to try to implement some of these dreams in practice; and one wonders whether the empirical approach is as common as we are apt to assume. But it is possible to be fairly confident about one thing, namely that Plato did not intend the *Republic* to be a manifesto for practical action. He may have thought that somebody, one day, could build a city like the one that Socrates describes; but not Plato, today. The city remains in heaven, in Cloud-cuckooland, almost in Never-neverland, waiting for the day when it can become actual. One reason for saying this is that it is essential, to Plato's conception, that the consent of the governed to the constitutional arrangements should be freely given. He quite explicitly does not want the rule of the philosophers to be imposed by force. He sees that there is a problem about how the consent of the governed is to be secured, but he offers no serious solution to it. At one point he proposes to secure it by a propaganda story which he cannot have expected anybody to take seriously. At another point he seems to envisage that it will be necessary for the population of his city, on its inauguration, to consist of children up to the age of ten—children still malleable enough to be taught to see the virtues of the regime. He cannot have supposed that this could actually be done. Again it is essential to his scheme that the rulers be philosophers and that the supreme rulers should have achieved the vision of goodness. But plainly he does not believe that any such rulers are as yet available.

He did not, then, suppose that the Republic which Socrates describes could actually be brought into existence then and there even if men of goodwill could be persuaded to attempt it. In discussing his proposals, however, Socrates is made to say that, even if his city cannot be achieved, nevertheless, if it is ideal, it will be well to try to approximate to it. This is a most dangerous principle. There are some things that are not worth doing unless they are done perfectly. That a *soufflé* is an excellent concoction does not mean that an approximation to a *soufflé* is preferable to similar ingredients served in the form of boiled eggs with bread and butter. Men of absolute wisdom, taking decisions in a community whose members concede the wisdom of the rulers, might be able to guarantee human welfare; men of less wisdom, governing those who do not concede their right to govern, will have to preserve their position by the force which Plato abhorred. At one level he was well aware of this; but one feels some uneasiness about the political crimes in which Plato might perhaps have been implicated in Syracuse had Dionysius proved an apter pupil. Others have started with the best intentions and produced the most disastrous results because they have failed to see that policies which might be admirable if they commanded general assent take on a very different form if they have to be imposed. If Plato had gone down this particular drain he would have done so against the force of his convictions; but there are precedents for that. Since, however, Dionysius' recalcitrance saved Plato from these temptations, it is useless to speculate whether he would or would not have been able, had things turned out otherwise, to extricate himself from the current in time. One can conjecture, however, that the comparative caution and realism of the political proposals in the *Laws* may be due to a realization, purchased in Syracuse, that it is irresponsible to advocate policies which you do not believe can be implemented without the use of methods which you think illegitimate.

Having outlined his ideal community, Socrates proceeds to describe how such a community might decline into corruption. Its decline is not foreseeable, but, because of the instability of mundane things, possible. The first step in the decline comes about when the rulers become careless of their role as upholders of the correct culture, and turn themselves into an aristocracy of power, or "timocracy" as Socrates calls it. Next they become an aristocracy of wealth, or "oligarchy". This is followed by democracy, which in turn gives way to tyranny (the tyrant being initially the popular leader against oligarchical counter-revolution).

Socrates and his friends (who, incidentally, are on this occasion Plato's elder brothers) are made to agree that each step in this process is a step downwards. Democracy, therefore, is worse that oligarchy and timocracy, and tyranny worse than democracy. Whether Plato really thought that democracy was worse than oligarchy is hard to say. He is much more venomous in his description of the oligarchic life than in his description of the democratic; and his belief in the power of wealth to corrupt should have made him dislike oligarchy very much indeed. He seems (oddly enough for one who had lived forty years or more of his own lifetime under democratic institutions, which had been vigorous long before his birth) to have supposed that democracy was essentially an unstable prelude to tyranny, and to have distrusted it on that score. There seems to be no class-sentiment in his dislike of democracy; the trouble is, rather, that under democratic institutions any proposal is liable to be accepted, and you never know where you are.

Nor is it easy to see whether Plato thought that in describing the decline from the ideal community he was describing how social change in fact takes place. Socrates is indeed made to give a plausible account of each of the transitions; and certainly Plato here offers some shrewd comments on the forces at work in society and in the individual. It seems, however, hardly likely that he can have thought that existing societies were the corrupt relics of primeval ideal communities—though he certainly sometimes plays about with ideas of golden ages in the remote past, cyclical recurrences in history, and other such fantasies. I am inclined to think, however, that Plato arrived at his order of merit between the degenerate societies, with democracy below oligarchy, as a result of trying to imagine a process of decline from the ideal, but that he did not seriously believe that such a process of decline had ever in fact taken place.[1]

Plato returns, years later, to the question of grading constitutions in the *Statesman.* He insists once more that the right way of conducting public affairs is that the ruling should be done by those who know how to do it; and he argues that in comparison with this point it does not matter whether there is one ruler or several, whether they are rich or poor, whether they rule with the consent of their subjects or without it. Such rulers, he insists, will not allow themselves to be bound by law; for law is a clumsy instrument which cannot take account of changed circumstances, nor of the variety of individual cases.

One supposes that Plato does not actually mean to say that a community could be well governed by a rich autocrat, ruling against the will of his subjects and without promulgating any laws. He presumably retains his distrust of wealth and his hatred of violence. Presumably also the philosopher who knows how to rule will share Plato's dislike of these things. Rather the point which Plato seems to be making in a rather infelicitous way is that what we as subjects need is good government, and that the question whether we get it or not depends on just one thing, namely whether the sovereign authority knows its business. In the light of that, nobody who is getting what he needs has any right to complain that he has not been consulted about it. That thinking men naturally form, and wish to express, opinions in public affairs does not seem to occur to him.

The philosophers in the *Republic* were fitted to rule partly because they knew all the answers, partly, however, because contemplating eternal verities makes a man incapable of entertaining trivial human ambitions. In the first capacity they were visionary beings who might at best exist one day; in the second

---

[1] The *Critias* believes, or pretends to believe, that a community like that described in the *Republic* had existed in Athens 9000 years ago.

capacity they were a present possibility. The *Statesman* seems to think that philosopher-kings are something which could presently exist if only people would see the good sense of allowing the wise to rule. But it concedes that people will not do this, and it argues that law, based on experience, is the substitute for the rule of the wise that some communities have devised. Constitutional government, in fact, is an "imitation" of one feature of the rational system of government-by-the-wise, since law is a clumsy imitation of insight. Unconstitutional government however is an imitation of the other feature of the rational system, namely of the philosopher-kings' supremacy over the law; and this is a disastrous imitation. If law is, at the best, a clumsy codification of understanding, the lawlessness of the foolish is a disastrous substitute for the wise man's right to do away with rules of thumb. We can divide political systems therefore into those which are constitutional or law-bound (which Plato seems to think implies the consent of the governed to the system), and those which are law-less, or unconstitutional. The former are to be preferred to the latter. Since the likelihood that a governing body will arrive at sensible decisions varies inversely with the size of the governing body, the best kind of constitution among those that are feasible in practice is constitutional monarchy; next to it comes constitutional upper-class rule, or aristocracy, followed by constitutional democracy. Since the likelihood of really bad government also varies inversely with the size of the governing body, the order of merit among the unconstitutional systems is the other way round; unconstitutional democracy is the best of them, unconstitutional upper-class rule, or oligarchy, the next, and unconstitutional autocracy or tyranny is the most vicious of all.

What Plato seems to mean by "law" is something like a common mind in society, as to how public affairs are to be conducted.[1] His essential point, therefore, is that inherited popular notions are certain to be crude and often exasperating, that they ought never to be allowed to stand in the way of genuine understanding, but that they are much to be preferred over the naked use of force, whether by popular assemblies, or by oligarchical cliques, or by single individuals. If you marry this principle with the principle that too many cooks spoil the

---

[1] The word *nomos*, or "law", does in fact connote something like this.

broth of deliberation, you arrive at the conclusion that the best results (in default of a philosopher-king) are to be looked for when one man takes the decisions under the general super-intendence of inherited notions of right and wrong. Plato does not seem at this stage to have reflected much upon Lord Acton's famous aphorism; as we shall see, however, it has some influence in the *Laws*. Nor, as we noticed earlier, does he realize that the political theorist, even in the ancient world, ought to be considering the government of societies that are not static, and in which new problems arise which the king, or the nobility, may not be well placed to understand. In so far as Plato's conception of politics is dynamic the dynamism is all on the political level; it is all a matter, in *Republic* 8 and 9, of how one system of government develops out of another. It does not occur to him that there might be such things as, for example, developments in trade or agriculture, leading to the necessity of legislative adjustments, and that in the making of these adjustments it might be expedient that those most affected by them should be represented. Law-making for Plato is always a matter of finding the right answer to perennial problems; apart from that the political problem is how to prevent the governing authority from committing blunders over day-to-day issues ranging from the treatment of individual citizens to the conduct of foreign policy. It would not occur to us to allow either treason-trials or declarations of war to be handled by popular assem-blies. It did occur to the Athenians, and Plato reasonably thought that this was no way to get the right answers. That there are other things involved in government Plato tended not to see. He had not reflected upon politics as profoundly as, for example, Thucydides. His indefatigable mind could not fail to consider political questions, and inevitably he made many shrewd observations. But it is difficult to believe that govern-ment was his chief interest. Mathematics, metaphysics and logic were more his *métier*.

Nevertheless the *Laws* is a remarkable achievement. It cannot be disputed that it is in parts very tedious to read, nor that it is often incoherently written. Plato must have been an old man when he began it; apart from the merits of the work there is something impressive in the idea of a man of seventy or so sitting down to draft in detail the whole of a legislative code from first principles. If in the *Republic* he had been unduly reluctant to descend from the level of generalities, here he most amply atones; he even tells us what we are to do with domestic animals that have taken human life. Undeniably some of Plato's worst delusions persist in the *Laws*, in particular the delusion that there is such a thing as just one kind of dancing, singing, poetry and the rest which can be allowed to play upon a man's imagination without corrupting him, with the corollary that no community can retain its health unless the wise men in it are given power to extirpate all cultural deviation. But at the same time we cannot withhold our admiration from the way in which Plato's humanitarian impulses have now in his old age overcome some of his most cherished ideas. We have seen that he never tolerated violence, but we have seen also that his distrust of most men's judgment led him to commend in his earlier writings constitutional arrangements which could only have been upheld by violence. The constitution recommended in the *Laws*, however, is as liberal as Plato's mania for cultural fixity will allow it to be. Weight has at last been given to the thought that your constitutional arrangements have to be such as to secure the consent of the governed.

The setting of the discussion is that the city of Cnossos in Crete is to found a colony at a place called Magnesia. A member of the committee which is to supervise the founding of the colony is talking with an Athenian and a Spartan friend. The Athenian gives the advice and the other two, for the most part, simply listen. It is insisted that nothing can go right in politics unless the pre-political foundations are correctly laid. The Athenian maintains in general that successful legislation requires a tyrant or autocrat to impose it; in practice in this particular case the mother-city of Cnossos is to act as the tyrant, and, the Athenian insists, is to see to it that certain conditions are satisfied from the beginning by the new foundation. It is not to be too near the sea; a cosmopolitan port is irredeemable. Nobody of bad character is to be allowed to join the new colony. There are to be rigid limits imposed on the amount of property a man can own, so that it is to be made impossible for any citizen to be very rich or very poor. No citizen is to be allowed to engage in manufacture; manufacture is to be in the hands of resident aliens. (The resident alien was a common Greek institution; he was a foreigner—a Corinthian, say, at Athens—living in a city other than his own as a free man but without membership of the citizen body). From the beginning the colony is to be given a legal code, and it is to have only limited power of amending it in the light of experience. From the beginning also the colony is to have officers and committees whose duty it is to see to it that corrupt forms of culture are forbidden.

In other words if you start off with a community consisting of the right sort of people living in the right sort of place, if you see to it that the right economic relations obtain between them, and that they are preserved from forces which exert an evil influence through the imagination, then you have a political problem which you can hope to solve. These things having been provided for the new colony, the Athenian goes on to propose for it a surprisingly enlightened constitution. He lays it down that no section of the community is to hold power; law is to be supreme. The various kinds of authority which exist in a community (that of parents, of the old, of the wise, of elected magistrates and so on) are to be played off against each other so as to secure the rule of law. Those who can live rightly and administer well without the rule of law are very rare indeed; most men, in such conditions, fall to the level of brutes. Evidently Plato has come to see that to hanker after all-wise rulers is to demand the moon; law is still a blunt instrument, but it is one which we have to employ. (He is even prepared to permit the courts to exercise a measure of discretion in order to offset the rough and ready nature of law). Having come to accept this point he is whole-hearted in trying to secure that no section of society can monopolize power. This he does by a system of checks and balances, and by complicated arrangements for the election of magistrates and other officers. He has a popular assembly, a senate chosen by a complicated system of popular election, a body of "guardians of the laws" (again chosen by popular election), and finally a supreme council (called the Nocturnal Council) consisting of senior officers and also of co-opted younger men. His officers (who correspond roughly to our cabinet ministers in their departmental functions) are chosen in various ways; some by a device which combines

N   183

popular election of candidates with the use of the lot to make the final choice, others by the votes of their colleagues. The distribution of functions between these various persons and bodies is difficult to follow, but it is clear that their variety is intended to prevent the dominance of any section of the community.

What would it be like to live in Magnesia? Some features of life there would be familiar to us. We should from time to time vote in elections. Officers whose conduct we disapproved of would be as difficult to get rid of as cabinet ministers from the point of view of the individual citizen. Public opinion would make itself felt in certain spheres, but its impact would be heavily cushioned and it would need time to take effect. We should find a state-maintained system of education for our children, administered by a minister of education chosen by the other magistrates to hold office for five years; but we should be surprised to find that the teachers were not citizens. We should find something approaching a judiciary. We should have our rights which nobody could infringe so long as we kept within the law.

We should not be involved in legislation. That in itself would not surprise us; what would be more unfamiliar is that broadly speaking nobody else would be engaged in legislating on our behalf. The guardians of the laws might from time to time correct an error in drafting which had come to light; but apart from that we should have inherited a comprehensive legal code from the foundation, and we should be looked at very askance if we wanted to see it modified. This would be almost as sinister as trying to introduce a new form of dancing, or a foreign practice of some kind. It would indeed be difficult to find out about foreign practices, for it would be difficult to get permission to travel. If we did get permission we should have to report back to the Nocturnal Council on our return, and this would be our opportunity for recommending the adoption of some practice we had seen abroad. The members of the Nocturnal Council would all have been put through a rigorous course of mathematical and philosophical training, and they were to be "the intelligence and the sense-organs" of the community. What we had found out by way of foreign novelty they would listen to in their capacity as sense-organs, and assess in their capacity as intelligence. If they pronounced against the new idea, we should be well advised to say no more about it.

The Good Society

The legal code under which we lived would have one surprising feature. This is that every law would be accompanied by an official "preface" explaining the theory underlying the law and trying to secure our rational assent to it. There would also exist "prefaces", or official declarations of the judgment of our founding fathers, on matters too minute or too intimate to be fit subjects for legal enactment. Under this part of the system we should find a grotesque organization of official matrons whose business it was to nip extra-matrimonial romances in the bud by speaking severely to those who seemed likely to offend in this way. We should find also that we could only contract marriages between certain ages, and that for ten years after marriage the disapproval of extra-marital liaisons would be particularly strict. Persistent offenders would be deprived of certain privileges such as that of attending weddings. If we were men we should be required to eat at common tables; the same demand would indeed have been imposed on women of all ages but for the invincible determination of this secretive race to conceal the amount that they eat and drink from the public eye. But it seems that after they have finished bringing up their families women also will mess in common. We should find that we were forbidden on pain of severe penalties from challenging the religious basis of the community, namely the doctrine that there are divine beings, that they make moral demands upon men, and that these demands cannot be sidetracked by sacrifices or other observances. We should be forbidden to indulge in any kind of private religious observances, on the ground that these encourage people to believe that the moral demands of the gods can be evaded. (Should we have had to imprison Socrates if he had lived in Magnesia? No, because the code is one to which he would probably have conformed; but some of his and Plato's Pythagorean friends might have been in trouble).

Parts of all this remind us of life in the Soviet Union—for example the difficulty of travelling abroad, or the existence of the Nocturnal Council as a sort of Communist Party having the duty of understanding and expounding the theoretical basis of the state. Parts of it remind us of life in the United States as Senator McCarthy would have liked to have it, with an elective system of government safeguarded by a firm ban on un-

The Good Society

American activities. But for the ordinary citizen who had no special enthusiasm for reforming the laws, and who could accept the culture of his society, life in Magnesia would have been quite tolerable. He would have been free from arbitrary arrest, he would have lived under a system of not inhumane law and order, and there would have been no risk of his being involved in the political faction-fighting which Plato took, probably rightly, to be one of the outstanding evils of Greek life. (If one lives under a political system in which it is difficult to keep oneself to oneself and to avoid being caught up in plots and counterplots, it cannot be very pleasant; and one would no doubt be more conscious than we can be, who have never known such conditions, of the virtues of living under a settled constitution). Life for the ordinary citizen of Magnesia must have been a bit like life for a middling man in Victorian England, except that the Magnesian would have done no work, other than on the land, and that he would have done a great deal more military service, physical training and the like, and would very possibly have had a better education.

The general criticisms that can be brought against the *Laws* as a contribution to political theory fall mainly into two kinds. Firstly Plato writes throughout under the influence of the assumption that it is possible to ascertain what are the best imaginative influences for men to live under, and that it is also possible to find the right answer to the conflicts which occur in society. On this assumption he naturally thinks that the political problem is: how to see that the right culture and right laws are enforced without giving too much power to those who are to do the enforcing. Given that this problem can be solved by the kind of division of power proposed in the *Laws*, Plato naturally supposes that there will be little recalcitrance on the part of the citizens to the maintenance of a regime which, after all, they will find works satisfactorily; and as for what recalcitrance there is, doubtless Plato would say, as any other political theorist except an anarchist says at some stage, that in the end the obstinate cannot be allowed to impede the well-being of the vast majority—particularly since, on the assumption that the cultural and legal dispositions are sound, the obstinate must be a hopelessly corrupt kind of man. One still feels inclined to argue that a thinking man will inevitably wish to exercise some

186

influence on public affairs, that Plato gives him little scope for doing so, and that he must in this way alienate the most valuable of his citizens. The best perhaps that can be done in mitigation of this criticism is to say that, with his essentially static conception of society, Plato would have tended to feel that there was not much that a man of good sense would wish to say on public affairs once the fundamental structure had been got right—and of course it is assumed that this has been done. A man of good sense would not want to change the structure; and if nothing else is changing in society, what other innovations could he wish to propose? The second sort of criticism that one can bring against the *Laws* is that Plato is still insisting on getting his pre-political foundations right before he will say anything about political action. To the man who wants to know how to proceed in a mercantile community, many of whose citizens are of poor moral fibre, and whose property-dispositions are grossly inegalitarian, what has Plato to say? Perhaps his message is: first try by whatever means (and you will probably need an autocrat) to get things right on this level; then you will be able to do sensible things on the level of political action. But it is hard to be sure of this. We ought of course in this context to remember that the practice of sending out colonies in the Greek world made it more natural for them than it is for us to try to find the recipe whereby, starting a new community from scratch, you could make it a lasting expression of happiness and justice. For a colony was a body of new citizens going to a new place to live under what could well be a new constitution. This, however, while it helps to explain Plato's approach to political theory, leaves it very largely irrelevant to those whose concern is with the maintenance of existing communities rather than the construction of new ones.

14

In Conclusion

THERE was recently in a national paper an article by an examiner in the General Certificate of Education. He had been marking General Papers, and very many of the candidates had answered the question: "Are young people today allowed too much freedom?". The examiner felt that there was an interesting measure of agreement between the various answers that he had read to this question; and the purpose of the article was to report what seemed to him to be the common attitude of this sample of young people to the problem of freedom and authority. Now nobody would dispute, I suppose, the legitimacy of writing an article of this kind, despite the fact that the article was essentially an act of interpretation. The author, that is to say, was trying to communicate to adult readers what seemed to have been going on in the minds of many adolescents; he was distilling the essence of hundreds of individual answers, and he was not presenting his distillation in the language or the form in which the answers had been written. Obviously, therefore, everything in the article was challengeable, and liable, also, to the charge of misrepresentation; for it reproduced in adult categories arguments, one essential feature of which was that they were not presented in those categories. Nevertheless it was an enlightening article.

Any account of the thought of Plato, or of any other philosopher who belongs to a culture alien to our own, must be in some ways like this. (The implication that Plato was a kind of intellectual adolescent must of course be discounted). If we want to interpret Plato to ourselves, we have to do so in our own terms, and these terms are not entirely his; in particular we have to be systematic, which he refused to be. So long as the conventions of representation are understood, this should not be thought of as misrepresentation. And yet there is perhaps a way in which a rather subtle misrepresentation is after all involved.

One can detect among philosophers two rather different conceptions of the nature and history of their discipline. According to a caricature of one view of the matter, the history of philosophy is comparable to the construction of a building. It progresses, though perhaps very slowly. Many modern exponents of the view would hold that some of the builders are careless, work too fast; and the bits that they contribute soon fall down. But if one is careful enough, if one is precise enough, if one spends enough time forging the technical terms, the logical distinctions, which are the tools of the trade, then brick by brick the building slowly rises; and one day, if we are patient enough, we shall have something to show for our labours—a bungalow perhaps alongside the sky-scrapers of mathematics and the sciences, but still a solid piece of construction. For things *can* be got right in philosophy; and once something has been got right, there it stands as an established result which can be built upon.

According to a caricature of the other conception, philosophy is more like a running skirmish. Nothing is ever established in philosophy, because the philosopher is a guerilla, and the enemy he is fighting against is also always on the move. The enemy is the propensity of human thought at any period to misconceive the results of its labours, to treat as closed many questions which are still open; and the function of philosophy is to destroy these misconceptions by raising awkward questions, by demanding explanations of what generally passes as current intellectual coin, by *franc-tireur* activities of every kind. In a way there are results, but the results are all ephemeral. The philosopher's contribution is to destroy the complacency of his contemporaries, to make them re-think what they thought had been settled, to force them to acknowledge that the established results of disciplined investigation do not really mean this or that, which they are currently taken to mean.

In Conclusion

The philosopher who holds the first conception will naturally value precision. He will attach importance to the development of logic, and to the formulation of a vocabulary of technical distinctions—even if that vocabulary is highly colloquial as such vocabularies nowadays often are. But the philosopher who is more interested in keeping open those questions which the trend of thought at the moment seems to have closed will not necessarily be so interested in precision; he will use it, but he will tend to use it *ad hominem*, in a particular intellectual situation, without much thought that he is sharpening a tool for others to use in different situations; and he will tend to suspect that the technical vocabularies of philosophers are themselves capable of concealing from us possibilities that ought not to be discounted. He will be inclined to disbelieve that there might one day be a terminology so precise and so philosophically neutral that anything that anybody might legitimately want to say could be clearly said in it.

Neither of these conceptions of philosophy and of philosophical method will do on its own. If we look at Plato in terms of the first conception we naturally think of him as a precursor—a precursor of Aristotle and therefore of Aristotle's successors. We think of him, as we have sometimes thought of him in this book, as the man who made the first moves towards getting clear the grammar of abstract thought, which Aristotle got rather clearer, and which it has been the business of his successors, and is still our business, to get clearer still. I have no doubt that it is legitimate to think of Plato in this way. We cannot do philosophy without a certain logical discipline, we cannot skirmish without weapons, penetration is not enough and clarity is indispensable. And without doubt the beginnings of clarity in the sphere of abstract thought are to be found, to all intents and purposes, in Plato, and are very substantial beginnings. Yet on the other hand we must not forget that Plato distrusted written philosophy, and believed in dialogue, that he did not believe that the truth could ever be written down in such a way as to preclude misunderstanding, that he held that seeing is always more important than saying. With one side of his mind, one feels sure, he would have admired the edifice of Aristotle's logic, formal and philosophical, he would have felt that Aristotle's Categories, for example, were an excellent set of tools for clarification, that the technical terms Aristotle coined were invaluable for drawing distinctions that one would sometimes want to draw. But with another side of his mind, one feels equally sure, the memory of Socrates' distrust of everything that is formulated would have made him wonder whether there was not a danger that every advance in clarity can be allowed to harden into a new rigidity. Why else was he himself so sparing in the coinage of technical terms, and also so unwilling to tell us in plain terms what his own opinions were? Take for example the conception of the beautiful which is obviously central to much of his thought. Why does he give us such very slender hints as to how he conceived of it? Was it timidity? Was he afraid that he would fail to formulate his meaning impeccably? But he was surely not a timid thinker. Do we not have to conclude that the reason was the reason that he so often suggests, namely that he did not value lapidary formulation, because no thoughts can be of value to anybody who has not thought his own way through to them? Understanding is displayed in intelligent performance in individual intellectual situations much more than in the production of precise definitions. The philosopher can usefully suggest but he cannot safely formulate. For what is formulated is always there, ready to be taken up and used by somebody who has not truly appropriated it, to whom therefore it will be an obstacle to further intellectual activity.

This perhaps is the chief value to us of Plato's philosophical writings, namely that their splendid vitality can serve to remind us that the wisest man in Greece, according to Apollo, was never satisfied that the last word had been said about anything.

That would have been a good note to end on. But it ought to be added that there is also something of value for us in Plato's more positive conception of philosophy. Though the midwife usually found that the ideas of which his clients wished to be delivered were imperfect and did not deserve to live, still the possibility always remained that somebody some day would give birth to one which was perfectly formed. When that happens, what it means is that one of the realities that we are familiar with in the dream of ordinary thought has been brought out into the day. Or in other words, what we are trying to do in philosophy is to achieve an explicit understanding of that which we understand implicitly all along; and the test of the goodness or otherwise of a philosophical theory is: does it help us to understand what we are doing when we think? As an account of the nature of philosophy, this is as good as any, and better than some.

Index

Academy, 1, 48
Akrasia, 148 sqq
Anamnêsis (recollection), 35 sq, 50
Apology, 17
Aristotle, 1, 8 sqq, 48 sq, 57, 84, 153
Art, ch 12
Astronomy, 68, 70 sq, 102

Beauty, 157, ch 12
Belief: *see Doxa*

Carroll, Lewis, 47 n
Category-mistakes, 19 sq, 40, 44, 84
Causal Theory (of perception), 93 sqq
Cave, simile of, 36 sq, 100 sqq, 135
Classes (*vs* properties), 44, 45, 121 sq.
Collection (*sunagôgê*), 41, 123 sq
Connaître (vs savoir), 106 sqq
Constitutions, relative merit of, 178 sqq
Copula, 44 sqq, 49, 53, 62, 120 sqq
Cratylus, 125 sq

Cratylus, 9
Creation, 23, 57, 66 sqq, 76, 80 sqq

Democracy, 172, 178 sqq
Dialectic, 38, 43, ch 9
Dionysius of Syracuse, 170
Division (*diairesis*), 122 sq
   dichotomous division, 126
Doxa chs 7 and 8, 140 sq, 169

Eleaticism; *see* Parmenides
Elements, (physical) 66 sq; (logical) 155 sq, 124 sqq
Embodiments (of forms), 62 sqq
Empirical (*vs* physical) world, 93 sq
Empiricism; *see* Locke, J.
Epinomis, 70, 82 sq
Erôs, 165
Eudoxus, 70, 153, 155
Euthydemus, 112, 140
Euthyphro, 138
Evil, problem of, 86

Fallacies, 6, 22, 111
False belief, paradox of, 112 sqq
Formal element (in forms), 57 sqq, 63

Index